ODENSE,
DENMARK

(TRAVEL GUIDE)

2025

Explore the City's Rich History, Cultural Attractions, and Natural Beauty

Christopher Levell

COPYRIGHT NOTICE

This publication is copyright protected. This is only for personal use. No part of this publication may be, including but not limited to, reproduced, in any form or medium, stored in a data retrieval system or transmitted by or through any means, without prior written permission from the Author / Publisher.

Legal action will be pursued if this is breached.

DISCLAIMER

Please note that the information contained within this document is for educational purposes only. The information contained herein has been obtained from sources believed to be reliable at the time of publication. The opinions expressed herein are subject to change without notice.

Readers acknowledge that the Author / Publisher is not engaging in rendering legal, financial or professional advice. The Publisher / Author disclaims all warranties as to the accuracy, completeness, or adequacy of such information.

The Publisher assumes no liability for errors, omissions, or inadequacies in the information contained herein or from the interpretations thereof. The publisher / Author specifically disclaims any liability from the use or application of the information contained herein or from the interpretations thereof.

Scan the QR-Code to see more books from the Author.

TABLE OF CONTENTS

CHAPTER 1: INTRODUCTION TO ODENSE 10
1.1. Welcome to Odense: A Brief Overview 10
1.2. Why Visit Odense in 2025? 11
1.3. A Snapshot of History, Culture, and Heritage 12
1.4. How to Use This Travel Guide 13

CHAPTER 2: HOW TO GET TO ODENSE 15
2.1. By Air: Nearest Airports 15
2.2. By Train: Rail Connections to Odense 16
2.3. By Road: Driving and Bus Options 17
2.4. By Ferry: Coastal Access Points 18
2.5. Tips for Hassle-Free Travel 19

CHAPTER 3: BEST TIME TO VISIT ODENSE 21
3.1. Seasonal Highlights: Spring, Summer, Fall, and Winter 21
3.2. Events and Festivals You Don't Want to Miss 23
3.3. Weather Considerations for Travelers 24
3.4. Ideal Duration of Stay 25

CHAPTER 4: PRACTICAL TIPS FOR VISITORS 27
4.1. Currency and Money Matters 27
4.2. Language Basics: Communicating in Danish 28

4.3. Health and Safety Tips 29
4.4. Internet and Mobile Connectivity 30
4.5. Packing Essentials for Odense 31
CHAPTER 5: TRANSPORTATION IN ODENSE .33
CHAPTER 6: TOP 10 TOURIST ATTRACTIONS 39
CHAPTER 7: CULTURAL AND HISTORICAL HIGHLIGHTS 51
CHAPTER 8: ACCOMMODATION IN ODENSE. 56
   A. Overview of Accommodation Options 56
   B. Luxury Resorts 57
   C. Budget-Friendly Hotels 57
   D. Boutique Guesthouses 58
   E. Unique Stays 58
   F. Top Recommended Accommodation 59
   G. Choosing the Right Accommodation for You . 59
   H. Booking Tips and Tricks 60
CHAPTER 9: WHERE TO EAT AND DRINK 62
CHAPTER 10: SHOPPING IN ODENSE 67
CHAPTER 11: ITINERARIES FOR EVERY TRAVELER 72
   A. Weekend Getaway 72
   B. Cultural Immersion 73
   C. Outdoor Adventure 74
   D. Family-Friendly Trip 75
   E. Budget Travel 76

F. Solo Traveler's Guide............77
G. Romantic Getaways............77
CHAPTER 12: FAMILY-FRIENDLY ACTIVITIES 79
12.1. Kid-Friendly Attractions............79
12.2. Parks and Playgrounds............80
12.3. Educational Experiences............81
CHAPTER 13: OUTDOOR ADVENTURES IN ODENSE............84
13.1. Cycling Routes and Trails............84
13.2. Parks and Nature Reserves............86
13.3. Boating and Water Activities............87
CHAPTER 14: FESTIVALS AND EVENTS IN ODENSE............89
14.1. Annual Celebrations............89
14.2. Music, Art, and Food Festivals............90
14.3. Local Cultural Events............91
CHAPTER 15: NIGHTLIFE AND ENTERTAINMENT............94
CHAPTER 16: DAY TRIPS FROM ODENSE........98
16.1. Exploring Funen Island............98
16.2. Visits to Nearby Castles............100
16.3. Coastal Escapes............101
CHAPTER 17: WHAT TO DO AND NOT TO DO 103
CHAPTER 18: PHOTOGRAPHY IN ODENSE...111

CHAPTER 19: ODENSE FOR BUDGET TRAVELERS 119
19.1. Free and Low-Cost Attractions 119
19.2. Affordable Dining Options 122
19.3. Money-Saving Tips 124
CHAPTER 20: SUSTAINABLE TOURISM IN ODENSE 128
CHAPTER 21: FREQUENTLY ASKED QUESTIONS 137
21.1. Common Concerns for First-Time Visitors 137
Do I Need to Speak Danish? 138
How Do I Get Around the City? 138
Is Odense Expensive? 139
What's the Weather Like? 139
21.2. Travel Hacks for Odense 140
CHAPTER 22: APPENDIX 144
A. Emergency Contacts 144
B. Maps and Navigational Tools 145
C. Additional Reading and References 146
D. Useful Local Phrases 147
E. Addresses and Locations of Popular Accommodation 148
F. Addresses and Locations of Popular Restaurants and Cafés 149
G. Addresses and Locations of Popular Bars and Clubs 150

H. Addresses and Locations of Top Attractions.151

I. Addresses and Locations of Book Shops..........152

J. Addresses and Locations of Top Clinics, Hospitals, and Pharmacies...............................152

K. Addresses and Locations of UNESCO World Heritage Sites...153

CHAPTER 1: INTRODUCTION TO ODENSE

1.1. Welcome to Odense: A Brief Overview

Odense, Denmark's third-largest city and the beating heart of Funen Island, is a place that effortlessly combines old-world charm with modern sophistication. As I stepped foot onto its cobblestone streets for the first time, I felt as if I had been transported into one of Hans Christian Andersen's timeless fairy tales. The city's allure lies in its ability to weave history, culture, and natural beauty into an enchanting tapestry that captivates every visitor.

Nestled amid verdant landscapes and charming waterways, Odense is a city that celebrates its rich heritage while embracing contemporary innovation. From its picturesque neighborhoods to its buzzing cafés and thriving art scene, Odense is a destination that promises something for everyone. Whether you're a history buff, a lover of the arts, a foodie, or simply someone seeking a tranquil getaway, this city is ready to welcome you with open arms.

1.2. Why Visit Odense in 2025?

Why should Odense top your travel list in 2025? Well, let me tell you, this year is shaping up to be an extraordinary time to visit. The city is pulling out all the stops to showcase its unique blend of cultural and historical offerings. Odense's calendar is packed with vibrant festivals, including the Hans Christian Andersen Festival, which transforms the streets into a living fairytale.

Moreover, the city is embracing sustainable tourism in innovative ways, making it a fantastic choice for eco-conscious travelers. In 2025, Odense continues to set an example for green living, with its extensive cycling paths, eco-friendly accommodations, and green spaces that invite you to reconnect with nature.

Not to mention, the city's culinary scene is flourishing like never before. With Michelin-starred restaurants, cozy bistros, and an emphasis on farm-to-table dining, Odense is a haven for food lovers. 2025 is also the year when new cultural landmarks, like the Andersen Museum expansion, are expected to open their doors, promising fresh experiences for returning visitors like me and first-timers alike.

1.3. A Snapshot of History, Culture, and Heritage

Odense is steeped in history, tracing its origins back over a thousand years. The name "Odense" itself derives from Odin, the Norse god, hinting at its deep Viking roots. Walking through the city, you'll feel the whispers of its storied past in every corner—from the medieval churches to the preserved half-timbered houses.

But history is only one layer of Odense's charm. The city's cultural significance is unparalleled. As the birthplace of Hans Christian Andersen, one of the world's greatest storytellers, Odense has an artistic soul that permeates every aspect of life here. Andersen's influence can be felt everywhere—from the museums dedicated to his life and works to the whimsical sculptures scattered throughout the city.

Odense's heritage isn't just confined to its past; it's alive and thriving in its present. The city boasts a vibrant arts scene, with theaters, galleries, and music venues that celebrate both traditional and contemporary creativity. Meanwhile, local traditions, such as Danish hygge, add a layer of warmth and hospitality that makes every visitor feel at home.

1.4. How to Use This Travel Guide

This guide is your key to unlocking the magic of Odense. Having spent countless hours exploring the city's nooks and crannies, I've poured my firsthand knowledge and personal experiences into this guide to help you make the most of your visit. Whether you're here for a weekend getaway or an extended stay, this guide will be your trusted companion.

I've organized the chapters in a way that takes you on a journey through Odense's many layers. From practical tips on transportation and accommodations to detailed itineraries for different types of travelers, this guide has you covered. You'll find recommendations for the best places to eat, drink, and shop, as well as insider tips to avoid tourist traps and discover hidden gems.

As you flip through these pages, think of me as your virtual travel buddy—here to share stories, offer advice, and ensure your trip to Odense is as memorable and enriching as possible. So, let's dive in and uncover the wonders of this remarkable city together!

CHAPTER 2: HOW TO GET TO ODENSE

Odense may not have the global fame of Copenhagen, but that's part of its charm. It's a destination that feels personal, like a treasure you've discovered on your own. Getting here, though, is as smooth as the Danish way of life itself. Allow me to share the best ways to make your journey to Odense effortless and enjoyable, no matter where you're coming from.

2.1. By Air: Nearest Airports

If you're flying into Denmark, your adventure will likely begin at Copenhagen Airport (Kastrup), the country's largest and most well-connected international hub. From here, Odense is a breezy two-hour train ride away. For those flying from nearby European cities, another option is Billund Airport, located about 100 kilometers west of Odense.

Copenhagen Airport is a marvel in itself—modern, efficient, and easy to navigate. After landing, you'll find direct train connections to Odense departing from the terminal, making it incredibly convenient to transition from the air to the rail. Billund Airport, on the other hand, offers a quieter experience and is closer to Odense by car or bus, making it ideal for travelers seeking a more relaxed route.

Flying into Denmark is the perfect prelude to your Odense journey. As the plane descends over Denmark's scenic landscapes, you'll catch glimpses of green fields, shimmering coastlines, and charming villages—offering a hint of the picturesque adventures that await.

2.2. By Train: Rail Connections to Odense

Ah, the Danish rail system—a thing of beauty and efficiency! The train is my favorite way to get to Odense, offering a seamless blend of convenience and stunning scenery. Odense is located on Denmark's main rail line, which means it's incredibly well-connected to major cities like Copenhagen, Aarhus, and even Hamburg in Germany.

The trains here are nothing short of luxurious. Spacious seating, free Wi-Fi, and large windows make the journey as enjoyable as the destination itself. If you're coming from Copenhagen, hop on one of the frequent InterCity or regional trains, which will whisk you to Odense in under two hours. The ride is smooth, and the countryside views—a patchwork of rolling fields, windmills, and quaint farmhouses—make it a journey to remember.

For those traveling from Hamburg or other parts of Europe, international train connections are equally reliable. Odense Station, a historic yet modern hub, is conveniently located in the city center, making it easy to step off the train and dive straight into your Odense adventure.

2.3. By Road: Driving and Bus Options

If you're someone who enjoys the freedom of the open road, driving to Odense is a fantastic option. Denmark's roads are immaculate, well-signposted, and a pleasure to navigate. From Copenhagen, the drive takes about two hours via the scenic E20 motorway, which includes crossing the awe-inspiring Great Belt Bridge. This engineering marvel connects Zealand to Funen and offers breathtaking views over the sea.

For a more eco-conscious choice, consider the bus. Long-distance buses, such as FlixBus, provide affordable and comfortable routes to Odense from cities across Denmark and beyond. The buses are equipped with Wi-Fi, charging ports, and reclining seats, ensuring a comfortable journey.

Driving also gives you the chance to explore charming stops along the way, such as Roskilde or the picturesque coastal town of Nyborg. Whether you're traveling solo or with family, the road to Odense is paved with opportunities for exploration and discovery.

2.4. By Ferry: Coastal Access Points

For travelers arriving from Scandinavia or Germany, ferries are a delightful way to reach Denmark. Although Odense itself doesn't have a port, you can dock at nearby coastal towns like Svendborg or Nyborg. These towns are a short drive or train ride from Odense and offer a unique maritime introduction to the region.

Ferry travel feels like stepping back in time, evoking a sense of adventure and connection to the sea. As you glide across the calm waters, you'll have a chance to enjoy the fresh sea breeze and panoramic views of Denmark's idyllic coastline. Ferries often accommodate cars, making them a convenient option for those combining sea travel with a road trip.

2.5. Tips for Hassle-Free Travel
To make your journey to Odense as smooth as possible, here are some insider tips:

- **Plan Ahead:** While Denmark's transport system is incredibly reliable, booking train and bus tickets in advance can save you money and guarantee your preferred schedule.
- **Travel Light:** Odense is a walkable city with excellent public transportation, so you won't need much luggage. Pack light to make your journey more comfortable.

- **Check Weather Conditions**: Danish weather can be unpredictable, so keep an eye on the forecast, especially if you're driving or taking a ferry.
- **Embrace Flexibility**: Sometimes the best adventures happen when plans change. Be open to exploring along the way, whether it's a cozy café in Nyborg or a stunning viewpoint on the Great Belt Bridge.

Getting to Odense isn't just about the destination—it's about the journey. Whether you arrive by air, rail, road, or sea, every route offers its own unique charm. So, choose the path that excites you most, and let the adventure begin!

CHAPTER 3: BEST TIME TO VISIT ODENSE

When I think of Odense, I see a city that transforms with each passing season, offering a kaleidoscope of experiences no matter when you visit. From the blooming vibrancy of spring to the cozy magic of winter, Odense always finds a way to welcome you with its unique charm. Let me guide you through the seasons, events, and perfect timing to make your trip unforgettable.

3.1. Seasonal Highlights: Spring, Summer, Fall, and Winter

Each season in Odense carries its own character, painting the city in different hues and atmospheres.

- **Spring (March to May):** Spring in Odense is nothing short of poetic. As the city awakens from winter, the gardens and parks burst into a riot of colors. Cherry blossoms line the streets, and you can hear birdsong in Munke Mose Park as you take leisurely walks. The Hans Christian Andersen Museum feels especially magical during this time, with the city's literary legacy blooming alongside nature.

- **Summer (June to August):** Ah, summer—when Odense truly comes alive. The days are long, warm, and perfect for exploring. Street festivals, open-air markets, and cultural events fill the calendar. I loved cycling along the Odense River or enjoying a picnic at Fruens Bøge Forest during these sun-drenched months.
- **Fall (September to November):** Fall is the season of golden leaves and crisp air. The forests and parks are drenched in autumnal hues, making it the ideal time for nature lovers. Odense's cultural scene thrives during this period, with art exhibitions and cozy cafés offering the perfect refuge from the chill.
- **Winter (December to February):** Winter in Odense is pure enchantment. The city sparkles with Christmas lights, and the markets are filled with the scent of mulled

wine and roasted almonds. One of my fondest memories is strolling through the cobbled streets of the old town, bundled up against the cold, feeling the magic of the season.

No matter the season, Odense promises an experience that feels both timeless and personal.

3.2. Events and Festivals You Don't Want to Miss

Odense thrives on its events, each one a celebration of art, culture, and community.

- **Hans Christian Andersen Festival (August):** This is a week-long extravaganza honoring the city's beloved son. The streets come alive with theatrical performances, fairy-tale reenactments, and musical concerts. It's an absolute must for families and fans of Andersen's timeless stories.

- **Tinderbox Music Festival (June):** If music is your passion, you'll love the vibrant energy of Tinderbox. Held in Tusindårsskoven, this festival attracts global and local acts alike, creating an unforgettable summer vibe.

- **Odense Flower Festival (August):** The city transforms into a floral wonderland during this event. Streets, sires, and even statues are adorned with intricate flower displays, making it a paradise for photography enthusiasts.
- **Christmas Markets (December):** Winter wouldn't be complete without the festive cheer of Odense's Christmas markets. The Hans Christian Andersen-themed market in the old town is a highlight, with stalls selling handcrafted gifts, local delicacies, and holiday treats.

Timing your visit around these events adds an extra layer of magic to your journey.

3.3. Weather Considerations for Travelers
Denmark's weather is known for its unpredictability, but it's part of the charm.

- **Spring:** Temperatures range from 5°C to 15°C (41°F to 59°F). Layers are your best friend during this season.
- **Summer:** Expect mild warmth, with temperatures hovering between 15°C and 25°C (59°F to 77°F). A light jacket for evenings is advisable.
- **Fall:** Temperatures cool down to 5°C to 15°C (41°F to 59°F). A waterproof coat is essential as rain showers become more frequent.
- **Winter:** Temperatures can dip to 0°C (32°F) or below. Bundle up with a heavy coat, gloves, and a scarf to enjoy the city's winter wonderland.

No matter the forecast, Odense's charm shines through—just be prepared, and you'll always be comfortable.

3.4. Ideal Duration of Stay

How long should you stay in Odense? Honestly, I could spend weeks here and still feel like there's more to discover. For first-time visitors, I recommend at least three to five days to soak in the city's highlights without feeling rushed.

- **A Weekend Trip**: Perfect for exploring the Hans Christian Andersen Museum, strolling through the old town, and enjoying a meal at one of the city's charming restaurants.
- **A Five-Day Stay**: Ideal for diving deeper into Odense's cultural and natural wonders. Add a day trip to Egeskov Castle or the Funen Village for a taste of the region's history.
- **A Longer Stay:** If you have the luxury of time, consider spending a week or more. This allows you to explore every nook and cranny, from the local markets to hidden hiking trails, at a leisurely pace.

Odense isn't just a destination—it's a city that invites you to slow down, savor, and truly experience its essence. Whether you're here for a weekend or a week, you'll leave with memories that linger like a favorite story.

CHAPTER 4: PRACTICAL TIPS FOR VISITORS

When planning your trip to Odense, having a few practical tips up your sleeve can transform your journey into a seamless and memorable experience. I've walked these streets, navigated its systems, and absorbed its rhythms, and now, I'll share what every traveler should know before arriving in this enchanting Danish city.

4.1. Currency and Money Matters

Denmark operates on the Danish krone (DKK), and while card payments are widely accepted, it's always wise to carry a bit of cash for smaller purchases or quaint markets. Odense, like much of Denmark, is remarkably modern when it comes to financial transactions—you'll find that credit and debit cards are accepted almost everywhere, even for a coffee or a bus ticket.

If you need cash, ATMs are conveniently located throughout the city. I found them easy to use, with English-language options available. It's worth noting that many Danish establishments don't accept

American Express, so a Visa or Mastercard is your safest bet. Keep an eye on your bank's foreign transaction fees, and consider using travel-friendly cards to save on extra costs.

4.2. Language Basics: Communicating in Danish

The beauty of visiting Odense is that most Danes speak excellent English, so you'll rarely encounter a language barrier. However, learning a few basic Danish phrases adds a touch of charm to your interactions and shows respect for the local culture.

Here are some essentials:

Hej! (Hi!)

Tak! (Thank you!)

Undskyld mig. (Excuse me.)

Hvor er…? (Where is…?)

Kan du tale engelsk? (Can you speak English?)

The locals always appreciate a warm "tak" after a meal or service, and I noticed it often led to broader smiles and friendlier conversations. If you're diving into Odense's museums or cultural spots, you'll find English translations almost everywhere, making it easy to enjoy the city's rich history and art.

4.3. Health and Safety Tips

Odense is one of the safest cities I've ever visited. Crime rates are low, and the locals are incredibly helpful, so you can stroll the streets at almost any hour with peace of mind. That said, it's always good to exercise standard precautions, such as keeping your belongings secure, especially in crowded areas or during festivals.

For healthcare, Denmark's system is top-notch. Pharmacies (apotek) are easy to find, and the staff are knowledgeable about over-the-counter remedies. If you require medical attention, hospitals and clinics in Odense are well-equipped, though it's essential to carry travel insurance to cover any unforeseen emergencies.

One tip: the Danish emergency number is 112, and for non-urgent medical advice, you can dial 1813. It's a comforting thought that help is always close by.

4.4. Internet and Mobile Connectivity

Odense, like the rest of Denmark, is a tech-savvy city were staying connected is effortless. Free Wi-Fi is available at most cafés, restaurants, and public spaces. Even the trains have Wi-Fi, making it easy to share your travel photos or check your itinerary on the go.

For extended stays, consider purchasing a Danish SIM card. I opted for one from Telia during my trip, but other providers like TDC, 3, and You See are equally reliable. These SIM cards often come with generous data plans, and they're available at convenience stores and mobile shops throughout the city.

If you prefer not to switch SIMs, check with your home provider about international roaming packages—it might save you the hassle of swapping cards mid-journey.

4.5. Packing Essentials for Odense

Packing for Odense requires a touch of practicality and a nod to the city's ever-changing weather. Regardless of the season, the Danish climate loves to surprise you. Here's what I recommend bringing:

Layers, layers, layers! Even in summer, mornings and evenings can be cool, so pack lightweight jackets or cardigans.

- Comfortable walking shoes. Odense's cobblestone streets and scenic parks are best explored on foot. A pair of sturdy yet stylish shoes will be your best friend.
- Rain gear. A compact umbrella or waterproof jacket is a must, as Denmark is known for its occasional rain showers.
- Adapters and chargers. Denmark uses the Type C and K plugs, so make sure your devices are compatible.
- Reusable water bottle. The tap water in Odense is clean, refreshing, and free, making it an eco-friendly and budget-friendly choice.

Finally, don't forget your camera or smartphone—you'll want to capture the storybook charm of this delightful city at every turn.

Preparing for Odense is about more than just packing bags and booking flights—it's about immersing yourself in its culture and rhythms. With these practical tips in mind, you'll feel less like a visitor and more like a welcomed guest in this remarkable Danish city.

CHAPTER 5: TRANSPORTATION IN ODENSE

Navigating Odense is not just about getting from one point to another; it's about experiencing the city's rhythm, immersing yourself in its daily life, and savoring its charm at every turn. This city, with its seamless blend of history and modernity, offers a range of transportation options that are not only efficient but also a pleasure to use. Let me take you through the ins and outs of moving around Odense like a seasoned traveler.

5.1. Public Transport: Buses and Trains

The public transport system in Odense is nothing short of impressive, combining reliability, affordability, and convenience. The city's buses are clean, punctual, and run frequently, making them an excellent way to explore the area. Tickets can be purchased through the FynBus app or directly from the driver, though buying in advance often saves you a few kroner.

One of my favorite aspects of Odense's public transport is its connection to the wider region. The train station, a bustling hub of activity, offers seamless rail connections to cities like Copenhagen and Aarhus. Trains are fast, comfortable, and equipped with Wi-Fi, allowing you to plan your next adventure while on the move. The scenic journey from Odense to Copenhagen is particularly memorable, offering glimpses of Denmark's lush countryside.

Pro tip: Opt for a Rejsekort, a rechargeable travel card, for hassle-free access to both buses and trains. It's cost-effective and eliminates the need for single-use tickets.

5.2. Bicycle-Friendly City: Renting and Riding

If there's one thing that truly defines Odense, it's the city's love affair with bicycles. Often referred to as Denmark's cycling capital, Odense boasts an extensive network of dedicated bike lanes that crisscross the city, making cycling not just a mode of transport but a way of life.

Renting a bike is incredibly easy, with options ranging from local shops to app-based services like Donkey Republic. I rented a bright orange Donkey bike during my stay, and it was one of the best decisions I made. Pedaling through Odense's charming streets, past half-timbered houses and tranquil parks, was pure bliss.

Whether you're gliding along the picturesque trails of Munke Mose Park or cycling to the iconic Hans Christian Andersen Museum, the experience is both invigorating and immersive. Don't forget to wear a helmet—it's not mandatory for adults but highly recommended for safety.

5.3. Taxis and Ride-Sharing Apps

For those moments when convenience takes precedence, taxis and ride-sharing apps come to the rescue. Taxis in Odense are safe and reliable, though they can be a bit pricey compared to other modes of transport. You can easily find them at taxi stands, major hotels, or by booking through apps like TaxiDanmark.

Ride-sharing services like Bolt and Uber aren't as ubiquitous here as in larger cities, but they're slowly making their presence felt. I found them particularly handy late at night or when carrying luggage. The drivers are friendly, and the cars are well-maintained, ensuring a comfortable ride every time.

5.4. Car Rentals and Driving Tips

If you're planning to explore beyond Odense's city limits, renting a car might be your best bet. Companies like Avis, Hertz, and Sixt offer a range of vehicles, from compact cars to spacious SUVs, catering to every type of traveler.

Driving in Odense is straightforward, with well-maintained roads and clear signage. However, be prepared for narrow streets in the older parts of the city, which can be challenging for larger vehicles. Parking is plentiful but often comes at a cost, so look out for designated parking areas or use apps like ParkMan to find the best spots.

A word of caution: Denmark enforces strict traffic rules, and speeding fines can be steep. Also, keep your headlights on at all times—it's the law, even during the day.

5.5. Walking Tours and Pedestrian-Friendly Routes

Walking in Odense is an absolute delight, thanks to its pedestrian-friendly streets and compact city layout. Many of the city's highlights, including the Hans Christian Andersen House and Brandts Klædefabrik, are within walking distance of each other, making it easy to explore on foot.

I recommend joining a guided walking tour to dive deeper into the city's history and culture. My tour through the historic district of Sortebrødre Torv was unforgettable, with stories of medieval monks and ancient markets bringing the cobbled streets to life.

For those who prefer a self-guided approach, grab a map from the tourist office or download a walking app. Don't miss the Odense River Walk, a tranquil route that meanders alongside the river, offering serene views and a chance to connect with nature.

Getting around Odense is more than a matter of logistics; it's an invitation to experience the city's soul. Whether you're zipping through on a bike, catching a bus, or strolling down its charming lanes, every mode of transport offers a unique perspective on this enchanting Danish city. With so many options at your fingertips, navigating Odense is a breeze— just pick the one that suits your mood, and let the adventure unfold.

CHAPTER 6: TOP 10 TOURIST ATTRACTIONS

Odense is a treasure trove of cultural, historical, and natural wonders. Its attractions range from fairytale-inspired museums to architectural marvels steeped in history. Exploring these sites is like peeling back the layers of the city's rich narrative, one enchanting discovery at a time. Let me take you through my personal favorites—the top five must-visit places that will leave an indelible mark on your journey.

6.1. Hans Christian Andersen Museum

No visit to Odense is complete without stepping into the world of its most beloved son, Hans Christian Andersen. The Hans Christian Andersen Museum is a poetic homage to the literary genius whose fairytales have enchanted readers worldwide. Walking into this museum feels like entering a storybook—whimsical and deeply immersive.

The museum offers more than just exhibits; it's an experience. From rare manuscripts and personal artifacts to interactive displays that bring Andersen's tales to life, every corner is a celebration of creativity. I was particularly taken by the multimedia installations that allowed me to "step into" his stories, feeling like a character navigating his imaginative worlds.

Don't miss the adjoining childhood home of Andersen, where his humble beginnings are vividly captured. As I stood in the tiny room where he spent his early years, I couldn't help but feel inspired by his journey from modest roots to international acclaim.

6.2. Odense Zoo

Odense Zoo is not just a place to see animals; it's a haven where conservation meets entertainment. Nestled along the scenic Odense River, the zoo offers a beautifully curated experience that's as educational as it is delightful.

The diversity of wildlife here is astounding. From majestic lions and playful lemurs to penguins waddling in their icy habitats, the zoo takes you on a journey across continents. My personal highlight? Feeding the giraffes during one of the daily interactive sessions—it was an unforgettable close encounter with these gentle giants.

For families, the zoo's Oceanium is a must-see. It showcases marine ecosystems with such vivid detail that you feel as though you're diving into the depths of the ocean. I also loved the African Savannah exhibit, where the open design allows animals to roam freely in a setting reminiscent of their natural habitat.

6.3. Egeskov Castle

Stepping onto the grounds of Egeskov Castle is like being transported into a fairytale. Located just a short drive from Odense, this 16th-century castle is a masterpiece of Renaissance architecture, surrounded by stunning gardens and shimmering moats.

The interiors are a feast for history enthusiasts, with rooms adorned with antique furniture, tapestries, and heirlooms that tell stories of the noble families who once resided here. One of the most intriguing features is the Titania's Palace, a meticulously crafted dollhouse that left me in awe of its detail and craftsmanship.

However, Egeskov is not just about history. Its sprawling gardens are a delight, with themed sections like the Labyrinth and the fragrant Rose Garden offering serene escapes. For adventure seekers, the treetop walk provides breathtaking views of the estate and beyond.

6.4. Brandts Art Museum

Art lovers will find their haven at Brandts, a contemporary art museum that combines visual spectacle with cultural depth. Housed in a former textile factory, the museum's industrial charm perfectly complements its cutting-edge exhibits.

Brandts features a rotating collection of modern art, photography, and design from both Danish and international artists. When I visited, I was captivated by an exhibit exploring the intersection of technology and art—a thought-provoking experience that lingered with me long after I left.

The museum also boasts a cinema and a charming café where you can unwind with a cup of coffee while reflecting on the art you've just experienced. Don't forget to check out the surrounding Brandts Passage, a vibrant area brimming with boutiques, galleries, and street art.

6.5. The Funen Village (Den Fynske Landsby)

To truly understand Odense's soul, a visit to The Funen Village is essential. This open-air museum is a living snapshot of rural Denmark in the 19th century. As I wandered through the reconstructed village, complete with half-timbered houses, lush fields, and farm animals, I felt as though I had traveled back in time.

What sets this attraction apart is its immersive approach. Costumed guides bring history to life by demonstrating traditional crafts like weaving and blacksmithing. I joined a group making traditional Danish butter—simple yet profoundly satisfying.

The village also hosts seasonal events, such as harvest festivals and Christmas markets, making it a dynamic experience no matter when you visit. The pastoral charm of this place left me with a deeper appreciation for Denmark's agricultural heritage and the way it has shaped the nation's identity.

Each of these attractions offers a unique perspective on Odense, weaving together the city's past, present, and future. Whether you're delving into the magical world of Hans Christian Andersen, exploring the artistic realms of Brandts, or simply soaking up the serene beauty of Egeskov Castle, you'll find yourself falling deeper in love with Odense at every turn. And these are just the first five—there's so much more waiting to be discovered!

6.6. Saint Canute's Cathedral (Odense Domkirke)

The towering spire of Saint Canute's Cathedral, or Odense Domkirke, rises majestically above the city skyline, beckoning visitors into a world of medieval wonder. Named after Canute IV, Denmark's patron saint and martyr king, this Gothic cathedral is both a place of worship and a historical treasure trove.

Stepping inside, I was immediately struck by the serene beauty of its vaulted ceilings and intricate stained-glass windows. The air seemed imbued with the whispers of centuries past, as though the very stones of the cathedral held stories of devotion, intrigue, and power.

The most profound moment of my visit was descending into the crypt, where the remains of Saint Canute and his brother, Benedict, rest in eternal slumber. It's a solemn, almost otherworldly experience, standing in the presence of such deep historical significance. Be sure to take a moment to admire the grand altarpiece and the organ, which produces hauntingly beautiful melodies during services.

6.7. Møntergården Cultural Museum

Møntergården is a museum that breathes life into Odense's rich past. Nestled in a picturesque courtyard, this cultural gem combines striking modern architecture with beautifully preserved historic buildings, creating a harmonious blend of old and new.

As I strolled through its exhibits, I felt as though I was piecing together the puzzle of Odense's evolution. The museum showcases everything from Viking artifacts to displays of daily life in medieval Denmark, painting a vivid picture of the city's journey through time.

One of my favorite parts was the children's area, which uses interactive displays and activities to make history engaging for all ages. For me, the highlight was an exhibit on the history of trade and craftsmanship, featuring intricate tools, textiles, and artifacts that showcased the ingenuity of Odense's ancestors.

6.8. The Danish Railway Museum

For anyone with a love of trains or a fascination with the industrial age, the Danish Railway Museum is a must-see. Located just a stone's throw from the central train station, this sprawling museum is an ode to the marvels of engineering and the transformative power of rail travel.

Wandering through the museum, I was like a child again, climbing aboard vintage locomotives and imagining what life must have been like for early train travelers. The collection includes everything from royal carriages to freight trains, each with its own unique story.

The interactive exhibits were a delight, offering a hands-on experience that even non-train enthusiasts would appreciate. I especially enjoyed the section dedicated to Denmark's role in the development of rail travel across Europe—it's a tale of innovation and perseverance that resonates deeply.

6.9. King's Garden (Kongens Have)

When I needed a moment of peace and reflection, I found solace in King's Garden (Kongens Have), a lush green oasis in the heart of Odense. This regal park, once part of the Odense Castle grounds, is a testament to the city's commitment to preserving its natural beauty.

Walking along its tree-lined paths, I was greeted by a symphony of birdsong and the gentle rustling of leaves. The garden's well-manicured lawns and vibrant flowerbeds create a serene atmosphere that's perfect for a leisurely stroll or a quiet picnic.

During my visit, I stumbled upon a small open-air concert, where local musicians played to an audience sprawled across the grass. It was a magical experience, blending music, nature, and the warmth of community.

6.10. Munke Mose Park

If King's Garden is the epitome of elegance, Munke Mose Park is its playful, laid-back sibling. Situated along the Odense River, this sprawling park offers a perfect blend of recreation and relaxation.

I spent an entire afternoon here, renting a paddleboat and gliding along the tranquil river while soaking in the park's scenic beauty. For families, the park is a haven, with playgrounds, open spaces for games, and even spots to feed the ducks.

What I loved most about Munke Mose was its accessibility and charm—it's a place where locals and tourists alike come together to unwind. The riverside paths are perfect for a leisurely bike ride or jog, and during the warmer months, the park hosts various events, from food festivals to outdoor yoga sessions.

These five attractions further cement Odense's status as a destination that offers something for everyone. Whether you're marveling at the grandeur of Saint Canute's Cathedral, immersing yourself in the city's history at Møntergården, or simply enjoying the natural splendor of its parks, each site adds a unique layer to the city's rich tapestry. My advice? Take your time to explore, and let Odense reveal its wonders at its own unhurried pace.

CHAPTER 7: CULTURAL AND HISTORICAL HIGHLIGHTS

Odense is a city where the threads of history and culture intertwine, weaving a rich tapestry that delights the soul of every visitor. Its cobbled streets and charming alleys speak volumes of a bygone era, while its vibrant cultural scene continues to evolve, honoring traditions while embracing modernity. Allow me to guide you through the captivating aspects of Odense's cultural and historical legacy, each of which has left an indelible mark on my heart.

7.1. The Legacy of Hans Christian Andersen

It's impossible to speak of Odense without invoking the name of Hans Christian Andersen, the world-renowned author and poet whose fairy tales have enchanted generations. Born in Odense in 1805, Andersen's life and works are inextricably linked to the city, and his presence is palpable in its very air.

During my visit, I found myself retracing Andersen's footsteps, starting with his humble childhood home, now a museum that brings his story to life. Wandering through the exhibits, I marveled at the relics of his life—worn quills, handwritten manuscripts, and illustrations of his tales. The museum's interactive displays allowed me to delve into his vivid imagination, exploring how his formative years in Odense inspired timeless tales like The Little Mermaid and The Ugly Duckling.

Walking along the Hans Christian Andersen Trail, I discovered statues, murals, and other tributes to the writer scattered throughout the city. Each one seemed to whisper a story, a reminder of his enduring influence not just on Denmark but on the world.

7.2. Traditional Danish Crafts and Arts

Odense is a haven for traditional Danish craftsmanship and artistry, where centuries-old techniques meet contemporary innovation. One of my most cherished experiences was visiting workshops and galleries where artisans still practice these time-honored crafts.

I spent hours in a pottery studio, mesmerized by the artist's hands shaping clay into elegant forms. Danish ceramics, with their minimalist yet functional designs, are emblematic of the country's aesthetic sensibilities. In another corner of the city, I watched a weaver at work, her loom clicking rhythmically as she created intricate patterns on soft textiles. These handwoven pieces are not just functional—they are pieces of art, steeped in history and tradition.

Odense's art galleries offer a vibrant counterpoint to its traditional crafts. At the Brandts Art Museum, I was captivated by exhibitions that juxtapose classical works with avant-garde creations. The city's burgeoning street art scene also caught my eye, with colorful murals adding a modern flair to its historic streets.

7.3. Key Historical Landmarks

Odense's historical landmarks are a testament to its enduring legacy, each one a chapter in the story of this remarkable city. From ancient castles to modern monuments, they offer glimpses into the lives of those who shaped Odense into what it is today.

One of the most striking landmarks is Egeskov Castle, a short drive from the city center. This Renaissance masterpiece, surrounded by a shimmering moat and sprawling gardens, feels like stepping into a fairy tale. As I wandered through its opulent interiors, I marveled at the period furnishings, intricate tapestries, and centuries-old artifacts that spoke of a life steeped in grandeur.

Closer to the heart of the city, I found Odense Castle, a less ostentatious but equally fascinating piece of history. Its understated elegance and beautiful grounds make it a favorite spot for quiet reflection.

For a deeper dive into Odense's past, I explored Møntergården, a cultural history museum housed in a beautifully preserved complex of buildings. Its exhibits, which range from Viking relics to medieval artifacts, transported me through the ages, offering a comprehensive view of Odense's evolution.

Odense is not just a city—it's a living museum, where every corner holds a story waiting to be uncovered. Whether you're drawn to the enchanting legacy of Hans Christian Andersen, the beauty of traditional Danish crafts, or the grandeur of its historical landmarks, Odense invites you to step back in time and lose yourself in its cultural and historical riches.

CHAPTER 8: ACCOMMODATION IN ODENSE

When planning a trip to Odense, choosing the perfect place to stay can significantly enhance your experience. During my time in this enchanting city, I explored a variety of accommodation options, each with its charm and distinct vibe. From luxurious retreats to budget-friendly havens, Odense offers something for everyone, ensuring a restful and memorable stay. Let me guide you through the diverse accommodation landscape to help you find your ideal home away from home.

A. Overview of Accommodation Options

Odense caters to a wide range of travelers, from those seeking opulent indulgence to backpackers on a shoestring budget. As I explored the city, I discovered an impressive array of accommodations, including grand resorts, cozy guesthouses, and unique stays that capture the city's essence. Whether nestled in the bustling city center or tucked away in tranquil neighborhoods, these options ensure comfort, convenience, and character.

B. Luxury Resorts

For those who revel in indulgence, Odense boasts several luxury resorts that redefine elegance. I had the pleasure of staying at one such property, where every detail, from plush bedding to gourmet dining, exuded sophistication. Resorts like these often feature spa facilities, lush gardens, and stunning views, offering a serene escape from the city's hustle and bustle. The impeccable service and attention to detail make these accommodations worth every penny.

C. Budget-Friendly Hotels

Traveling on a budget doesn't mean compromising on comfort in Odense. The city is peppered with budget-friendly hotels that provide clean, cozy rooms and essential amenities at reasonable prices. During one of my visits, I stayed in a charming little hotel where the staff's warmth made me feel right at home. Many of these establishments are conveniently located near public transport, making it easy to explore Odense without breaking the bank.

D. Boutique Guesthouses

There's something uniquely personal about boutique guesthouses in Odense. I remember staying in a quaint guesthouse with just a handful of rooms, each thoughtfully designed with Danish hygge in mind. The intimate setting allowed me to connect with fellow travelers and the host, who shared insider tips on the best local spots. These guesthouses often reflect the city's artistic and cultural vibe, making them an excellent choice for those who appreciate individuality and charm.

E. Unique Stays

If you're looking for something out of the ordinary, Odense doesn't disappoint. I once stayed in a converted windmill just outside the city—a truly unforgettable experience! From historic buildings with modern interiors to eco-friendly lodges surrounded by nature, these unique stays offer a fresh perspective on Odense's diverse heritage and innovation.

F. Top Recommended Accommodation

To simplify your search, here are my top recommendations based on my stays and feedback from fellow travelers:

- **Hotel Odeon**: A sleek and modern hotel in the city center, perfect for luxury seekers.
- **City Hotel Odense**: A budget-friendly gem with excellent amenities and a central location.
- **Amalie Bed & Breakfast**: A cozy boutique guesthouse offering personalized service.
- **Egeskov Castle Stay**: Experience royal living in this historic castle's guest accommodations.

G. Choosing the Right Accommodation for You

Selecting the ideal place to stay depends on your preferences and travel style. If you're visiting with family, look for spacious options with kid-friendly amenities. Solo travelers might appreciate the social atmosphere of a boutique guesthouse, while couples can enjoy the privacy and romance of a luxury resort.

For adventurers, unique stays can add an extra layer of excitement to your journey.

H. Booking Tips and Tricks

Booking accommodation in Odense requires a bit of strategy, especially during peak seasons. Here are some tips I've learned along the way:

- **Book Early:** Popular spots fill up quickly, especially during festivals and holidays.
- **Use Trusted Platforms**: Websites like Booking.com or Airbnb offer reliable options with reviews.
- **Check Cancellation Policies**: Flexibility is key if your plans might change.
- **Look for Deals**: Keep an eye out for seasonal discounts and special packages.

Odense's accommodations are as diverse as the city itself, offering something for every taste and budget. Whether you're unwinding in a luxurious spa, mingling in a boutique guesthouse, or soaking in the charm of a unique stay, the city ensures you feel at home. So, pack your bags and let Odense's warm hospitality welcome you!

CHAPTER 9: WHERE TO EAT AND DRINK

One of the greatest joys of traveling is immersing oneself in the culinary delights of a destination, and Odense is a treasure trove for food lovers. The city's dining scene is a vibrant tapestry woven with traditional Danish flavors, international cuisines, and innovative gastronomic creations. Having explored its restaurants, cafés, and markets during my visits, I can confidently say that Odense caters to every palate. Let me guide you through its culinary landscape, from hearty smørrebrød to cozy cafés and buzzing food markets.

9.1. Traditional Danish Cuisine

When in Odense, savoring traditional Danish cuisine is an absolute must. The heart and soul of Danish gastronomy lie in its simplicity and focus on fresh, local ingredients. I fondly remember my first taste of smørrebrød, Denmark's beloved open-faced sandwich. Each bite was a medley of textures and flavors—rye bread topped with herring, fresh dill, and a tangy mustard dressing.

Don't miss out on frikadeller (Danish meatballs), æbleskiver (delicious pancake balls), or the comforting warmth of flæskesteg (roast pork with crispy crackling). Many restaurants in Odense pay homage to these timeless dishes, and the experience feels like a journey through Denmark's culinary history.

9.2. Top Restaurants and Cafés

Odense is home to an impressive array of restaurants and cafés, each offering something unique. During my stay, I fell in love with Sortebro Kro, a charming restaurant set in a historic building, where traditional dishes are served with a modern twist. For a fine-dining experience, I recommend Restaurant Under Lindetræet, nestled near Hans Christian Andersen's house. The ambiance and flavors are truly magical, much like the fairy tales written nearby.

For a more casual vibe, head to Café Skt. Gertrud, a local favorite that exudes warmth and charm. The coffee is divine, and their pastries rival anything you'd find in Copenhagen. On a sunny day, grab an outdoor seat and watch the world go by.

9.3. Street Food Spots and Markets

If you're seeking a more informal dining experience, Odense's Street food scene won't disappoint. The Storms Pakhus, a vibrant food market located in an old warehouse, quickly became one of my favorite spots. It's a bustling hub where you can sample flavors from around the world, from spicy Thai curries to Italian wood-fired pizzas.

The market's lively atmosphere is infectious, and it's a fantastic place to mingle with locals and fellow travelers. I also stumbled upon pop-up stalls offering pølser (Danish hot dogs) with all the trimmings—a quick, satisfying bite while exploring the city.

9.4. Best Bars and Pubs

When night falls, Odense transforms into a lively hotspot for socializing and unwinding. I discovered a variety of bars and pubs that cater to different vibes, whether you're in the mood for craft cocktails, local beer, or a cozy corner to sip on a glass of wine.

Bryggeriet Flakhaven, a brewery and bar located in the city center, serves some of the best craft beers I've tasted. Their seasonal brews are a treat for beer enthusiasts. For a more elegant evening, I recommend Bar Snik Snak, known for its creative cocktails and intimate setting.

If you're craving a more traditional pub experience, The Tipsy Toad will transport you to an old-world British pub right in the heart of Odense.

9.5. Vegetarian and Vegan Dining Options

As a city that embraces modern dining trends, Odense caters wonderfully to vegetarian and vegan travelers. I was delighted to find a growing number of eateries that prioritize plant-based options without compromising on flavor.

Plant Food was a standout, offering a vibrant menu filled with dishes like colorful Buddha bowls and hearty vegan burgers. I also loved Den Grønne Papaya, a restaurant blending Asian and Danish influences to create vegetarian-friendly delights.

For a quick, guilt-free snack, many cafés offer vegan pastries and dairy-free lattes—a perfect pick-me-up during a day of sightseeing.

Odense is a culinary playground, where every meal tells a story and every dish reflects the city's rich heritage and cosmopolitan spirit. Whether you're indulging in traditional Danish fare, exploring global flavors at a food market, or unwinding at a cozy café, the city promises an unforgettable gastronomic adventure. So, loosen your belt, follow your nose, and let Odense tantalize your taste buds in ways you never imagined.

CHAPTER 10: SHOPPING IN ODENSE

Shopping in Odense is more than just a transaction—it's an experience, a delightful immersion into the city's artistry, culture, and local life. Whether you're hunting for handcrafted treasures, exploring bustling markets, or strolling down charming shopping streets, Odense offers a variety of options to satisfy every shopper's heart. Let me walk you through the retail gems I discovered during my time in this enchanting city.

10.1. Souvenirs and Handcrafted Goods

When it comes to souvenirs, Odense is a haven for unique, meaningful keepsakes that reflect its rich history and cultural heritage. During my explorations, I found that handcrafted items reign supreme here. For fans of Hans Christian Andersen, like myself, there's no shortage of memorabilia inspired by his timeless fairy tales. From beautifully illustrated books to whimsical figurines of characters like the Little Mermaid or the Ugly Duckling, these make for wonderful mementos.

The local artisans in Odense also craft exquisite ceramics, textiles, and jewelry, each piece bearing the signature of Danish craftsmanship. I particularly loved the handwoven scarves and pottery adorned with intricate Nordic designs—both are not only beautiful but also functional gifts.

If you're looking for something truly authentic, pay a visit to Fynsk Kunsthåndværk, where you'll find a curated selection of artisan creations from across the Funen region. It's a treasure trove of handmade goods that reflect the soul of Odense.

10.2. Top Shopping Streets and Malls

Odense's shopping streets are like open-air galleries, blending retail therapy with picturesque surroundings. My favorite street for a leisurely shopping spree was Kongensgade, a lively pedestrian avenue lined with a mix of global brands and independent boutiques. Whether you're on the hunt for chic Danish fashion, high-end cosmetics, or trendy accessories, this street has it all.

For a more eclectic vibe, head to Vestergade, where quaint shops and cozy cafés create an inviting atmosphere. I stumbled upon a delightful store called Storms Boutique, which offers an array of vintage finds and quirky collectibles. Every corner of Vestergade seems to have a story waiting to be discovered.

If you prefer an all-under-one-roof shopping experience, Rosengårdcentret, Odense's largest shopping mall, is a must-visit. With over 150 stores, including international brands and Danish designers, it's a shopper's paradise. The mall also boasts excellent dining options, making it a perfect spot to recharge after a busy day of retail therapy.

10.3. Local Markets and Boutiques

For me, nothing captures the spirit of a city quite like its local markets, and Odense's markets are no exception. The Odense Market Hall was a personal favorite—a bustling space filled with fresh produce, gourmet delicacies, and artisan goods. Strolling through the stalls, I found everything from organic cheeses and cured meats to fragrant flowers and handmade candles.

If you visit on a weekend, make time for the Farmer's Market in the heart of the city. It's a vibrant gathering of local vendors offering everything from farm-fresh fruits to handcrafted soaps. I spent hours chatting with the friendly stall owners and sampling regional specialties like freshly baked rye bread and honey straight from the hive.

For boutique shopping, Odense's hidden gems shine brightest. Stores like Mette Guldberg Design and Sinnerup showcase Scandinavian minimalism at its finest, with home décor, clothing, and accessories that exude understated elegance. These boutiques are perfect for finding one-of-a-kind items that embody Danish style and sophistication.

Shopping in Odense is an adventure in itself—a chance to connect with the city's creative spirit and take home a piece of its charm. Whether you're browsing artisan markets, exploring chic boutiques, or strolling through vibrant shopping streets, the experience is as rewarding as the treasures you'll uncover. So, set aside some time, let your curiosity guide you, and allow Odense's retail wonders to captivate you.

CHAPTER 11: ITINERARIES FOR EVERY TRAVELER

One of the most delightful aspects of Odense is its versatility—it's a city that caters to every kind of traveler. Whether you're here for a quick weekend escape, a deep dive into Danish culture, or a romantic retreat, Odense offers experiences that are as unique as its visitors. Having spent ample time exploring this enchanting city, I've curated itineraries to help you make the most of your stay, tailored to your preferences and travel style.

A. Weekend Getaway

If you've only got a couple of days, don't worry—Odense's charm can be savored even in a short visit. Start your Saturday morning at the Hans Christian Andersen Museum, immersing yourself in the life and works of Denmark's beloved storyteller. Grab a light brunch at Nelle's Coffee & Wine, where the cozy ambiance sets the tone for a relaxing day.

In the afternoon, stroll through the King's Garden (Kongens Have) and visit Saint Canute's Cathedral to admire its Gothic architecture. Wrap up your day with a dinner at Sortebro Kro, a Michelin-recommended restaurant that serves modern Nordic cuisine with a historical twist.

On Sunday, enjoy a leisurely walk at Munke Mose Park and then explore the Odense Zoo, which is perfect for visitors of all ages. Before you leave, swing by the Brandts Art Museum for a dose of contemporary art and culture.

B. Cultural Immersion

Odense is a city steeped in culture, and if you're a lover of history and the arts, this itinerary is for you. Begin your exploration at The Funen Village (Den Fynske Landsby), an open-air museum that recreates life in a 19th-century Danish village. Walking through the cobblestone paths, I felt transported to another era, surrounded by thatched-roof houses and vibrant reenactments.

Spend your afternoon at Møntergården, Odense's cultural history museum, where exhibits showcase everything from Viking artifacts to the city's evolution. In the evening, treat yourself to a performance at Odense Teater, one of Denmark's oldest theaters. The productions here are nothing short of mesmerizing.

On your second day, join a guided walking tour focused on Hans Christian Andersen's life, visiting his childhood home and other significant landmarks. Complete your cultural immersion with a visit to Egeskov Castle, a breathtaking Renaissance-era estate just outside the city.

C. Outdoor Adventure

For those who find solace in nature, Odense is a hidden gem of outdoor escapes. Start your day with a bike ride along the Odense River Path, a picturesque trail that meanders through parks and lush greenery. Renting a bicycle is easy in this bike-friendly city, and it's the best way to soak in the natural beauty.

Pack a picnic and head to Munke Mose Park, where the serene surroundings provide a perfect backdrop for a leisurely lunch. If you're up for more adventure, visit the Odense Fjord, a short drive away, where you can kayak or birdwatch.

Wrap up your day at King's Garden, which offers a peaceful retreat with beautifully manicured lawns and vibrant flower beds. For longer stays, consider venturing to the nearby Svanninge Hills, known for its hiking trails and panoramic views.

D. Family-Friendly Trip

Traveling with kids? Odense has plenty to keep little ones entertained. Start at the Odense Zoo, which features interactive exhibits and a diverse array of animals. My favorite part was the penguin enclosure—watching their antics is a joy for both children and adults.

In the afternoon, head to The Danish Railway Museum, where kids can climb aboard historic trains and even participate in hands-on activities. Don't miss the museum's outdoor playground—it's a hit with younger visitors.

For dinner, opt for Olivia Brasserie, a family-friendly restaurant offering a variety of dishes that cater to all tastes. On your second day, spend time at The Funen Village, where the immersive experience of historical Denmark will captivate children and adults alike.

E. Budget Travel

Odense proves that you don't need to splurge to have an unforgettable time. Start your day with a free walking tour of the city, which covers major landmarks and gives insight into Odense's rich history. Pack a lunch from a local supermarket and enjoy it at Munke Mose Park, a cost-free yet picturesque spot.

Visit Saint Canute's Cathedral, where entry is free, and admire its stunning interior. Another budget-friendly option is the Odense Public Library, which often hosts free cultural events and exhibitions.

For dinner, check out the food stalls at Storms Pakhus, Odense's Street food market, where you can savor delicious meals without breaking the bank. On your second day, explore the open-air exhibits at The Funen Village, which often has discounted entry fees during off-peak times.

F. Solo Traveler's Guide

Traveling solo in Odense is a liberating experience, filled with opportunities for self-discovery. Begin your day with a quiet morning at the Hans Christian Andersen Museum, followed by a leisurely coffee at Kafferiet.

In the afternoon, lose yourself in the serene beauty of Odense River Path, either on foot or by bike. This trail offers plenty of scenic spots for quiet reflection. Dinner at Mmoks, known for its fusion cuisine, is a great way to treat yourself.

On your second day, join a group tour of Egeskov Castle—a great way to meet fellow travelers—and spend the afternoon exploring its beautiful gardens. Don't forget to end your journey with some self-care at a local spa, such as H. C. Andersen Spa, which offers relaxing treatments inspired by the fairy tales.

G. Romantic Getaways

Odense is undeniably romantic, with its fairytale charm and intimate settings. Begin your getaway with a horse-drawn carriage ride through the city, followed by a visit to Egeskov Castle, where you can wander hand-in-hand through its stunning gardens.

Book a table at Restaurant Under Lindetræet, located in a historic building near the Hans Christian Andersen Museum. The candlelit ambiance and exquisite cuisine make it perfect for couples.

On your second day, take a private boat ride along the Odense River, enjoying the tranquility and beautiful scenery. For a unique date, visit Brandts Art Museum, where you can discuss your favorite pieces and create shared memories. End your trip with a stroll through King's Garden, especially magical at sunset.

Odense's charm lies in its ability to cater to every traveler's needs and preferences. Whether you're here for adventure, culture, romance, or family fun, this city promises unforgettable experiences that you'll carry with you long after you leave. Let these itineraries guide you, but remember—the best moments often come from wandering off the beaten path. Happy travels!

CHAPTER 12: FAMILY-FRIENDLY ACTIVITIES

Odense is a treasure trove of family-friendly activities that keep everyone entertained, from curious toddlers to energetic teens—and even the grown-ups! I've explored this city with my family and can vouch for the countless ways Odense creates magical moments for families. It's a place where history, fun, and nature intertwine beautifully to offer something for everyone.

12.1. Kid-Friendly Attractions

Odense Zoo is the ultimate destination for families, and trust me, your kids will adore it. I remember the look of awe on my little one's face when we watched the giraffes strut gracefully across their enclosure. The penguin habitat is an absolute highlight; it's hard not to chuckle at their playful antics. The zoo also has a petting area where children can interact with goats and other animals—a hands-on experience that always leaves them giggling.

Another must-visit is the Danish Railway Museum. My children couldn't get enough of the vintage train carriages, and I found myself equally captivated by the nostalgia of it all. They even have kid-sized trains that children can ride, making it a truly immersive experience. The museum's play area is perfect for burning off some energy while you take a breather.

For something a bit whimsical, head to the Hans Christian Andersen Museum. It's not just an educational spot—it's a gateway to a magical world. The interactive exhibits bring his beloved fairy tales to life, captivating young minds. My kids were thrilled to see scenes from The Ugly Duckling and The Little Mermaid depicted so vividly.

12.2. Parks and Playgrounds

Odense is dotted with lush parks and playful spaces, making it an outdoor haven for families. Munke Mose Park quickly became one of our favorites. There's a lovely play area where kids can climb, swing, and slide to their hearts' content, while parents relax on nearby benches under the shade of towering trees. On warm days, we rented a paddleboat and floated lazily along the river—a simple yet delightful activity that brought endless giggles.

Another gem is King's Garden (Kongens Have), where the manicured lawns and colorful flowerbeds make for an idyllic picnic spot. We spread out a blanket, enjoyed some pastries we'd picked up from a local bakery, and watched as our kids chased each other across the open space. There's something so charming about letting kids run free in a space that feels like it belongs in a storybook.

For those with younger children, the Odense River Path offers a gentle walking trail perfect for strollers. Along the way, we stumbled upon small hidden playgrounds and scenic spots that were ideal for short breaks.

12.3. Educational Experiences

Odense offers plenty of opportunities to combine fun with learning, ensuring that your trip is both entertaining and enriching. The Funen Village (Den Fynske Landsby) is a standout. As we wandered through this open-air museum, the kids were fascinated by costumed interpreters demonstrating traditional Danish crafts. They even got to try their hand at butter churning and candle making! It's a fantastic way to introduce children to history in an engaging and interactive setting.

Another enriching activity is a visit to Møntergården, a cultural museum that's both educational and kid-friendly. My older child loved the Viking exhibits, while the younger one was engrossed in the interactive displays designed just for kids. The museum's storytelling sessions are a treat, weaving tales that capture the imagination of children and adults alike.

For a truly unique experience, consider a workshop at the Odense Science Center. This hidden gem offers hands-on activities that teach kids about science, technology, and sustainability. I still remember the joy on my son's face as he built a miniature wind turbine and watched it spin for the first time. It's the kind of place where curiosity is sparked, and lifelong interests are born. Odense is a city that truly understands the joy of family travel.

Every corner seems to invite exploration, laughter, and bonding moments. From enchanting fairy tale settings to hands-on educational experiences, the city ensures that your family trip will be nothing short of magical. Watching my children's faces light up at every turn made me fall even more in love with this charming destination. If you're traveling as a family, Odense won't just meet your expectations—it will exceed them in ways you'll cherish forever.

CHAPTER 13: OUTDOOR ADVENTURES IN ODENSE

Odense is an enchanting blend of urban charm and natural beauty, offering outdoor adventures that cater to every type of traveler. I've spent countless hours exploring its cycling paths, serene parks, and glistening waterways, and each experience has deepened my appreciation for the city's dedication to preserving its natural allure. Whether you're a nature enthusiast, an adventure seeker, or someone looking to unwind, Odense has a plethora of outdoor activities that will invigorate your spirit.

13.1. Cycling Routes and Trails

If there's one thing that stands out about Odense, it's how much this city loves its bicycles. Known as Denmark's cycling capital, Odense is crisscrossed by a network of bike-friendly routes that make exploring its nooks and crannies an absolute delight. During my visits, I found cycling not only the most efficient way to get around but also the most immersive.

One of my favorite routes is the Odense River Path, a tranquil trail that meanders alongside the gentle river. This path takes you through lush greenery, past charming bridges, and alongside picturesque picnic spots. It's an easy ride suitable for families and novice cyclists, yet it still offers stunning vistas that keep experienced riders captivated.

For those craving a bit more adventure, the Hesbjerg Forest Trail is a must-try. This route takes you through dense woodlands, where the rustle of leaves and the chirping of birds form a soothing soundtrack to your ride. I remember feeling like I'd stepped into a fairytale as I pedaled through this enchanting forest.

Odense's commitment to cycling is evident in its bike rental services, which are both affordable and convenient. Whether you're renting from a local shop or using one of the city's bike-share programs, you'll find it easy to hit the trails and explore at your own pace.

13.2. Parks and Nature Reserves

Odense's parks are a testament to its love for green spaces, and they've become my personal sanctuaries whenever I need to escape the hustle and bustle of the city. Munke Mose Park is a favorite of mine, with its sprawling lawns, flower-filled gardens, and serene riverside walkways. It's a perfect spot for a leisurely afternoon, whether you're lounging on the grass with a book or taking a gentle stroll along the water.

For a more immersive nature experience, I recommend visiting Stige Island, a hidden gem that feels worlds away from urban life. This nature reserve offers walking trails, birdwatching spots, and breathtaking views of the surrounding wetlands. I've spent countless hours here, soaking in the tranquility and marveling at the diverse wildlife.

Another standout is The Funen Alps, a charmingly misnamed area with gentle hills and stunning landscapes. It's a great spot for hiking, and the panoramic views from the top are worth every step. I'll never forget the feeling of standing at the summit, breathing in the fresh air, and marveling at the rolling countryside below.

13.3. Boating and Water Activities

The waterways of Odense add a unique charm to the city, offering opportunities for boating and other water-based activities that are both relaxing and invigorating. One of the most memorable experiences I've had was renting a paddleboat at Munke Mose Park and gliding lazily down the Odense River. It's a serene way to take in the scenery, with willow trees dipping their branches into the water and ducks swimming alongside you.

If you're looking for something more adventurous, consider a kayak tour along the river. These guided tours provide a unique perspective of Odense, taking you past iconic landmarks and hidden corners that are best appreciated from the water. I vividly remember the peacefulness of paddling under the canopy of trees, with the city's vibrant energy just a stone's throw away.

For families or those who prefer a more relaxed pace, there are river cruises that offer a leisurely journey through Odense's waterways. These cruises often include commentary about the city's history and landmarks, making them both entertaining and educational.

Odense's outdoor adventures are a celebration of its natural beauty and vibrant lifestyle. From cycling through scenic trails to exploring tranquil parks and enjoying the gentle flow of its waterways, every experience in the city feels like a breath of fresh air. I've come to cherish these moments of connection with nature, and I'm certain you will too. Whether you're seeking thrills, serenity, or simply a new perspective, Odense's great outdoors have something magical in store for you.

CHAPTER 14: FESTIVALS AND EVENTS IN ODENSE

Odense, the heart of Funen, is not just a city of enchanting cobblestone streets and fairy-tale charm; it is also a vibrant hub of festivals and events that celebrate its rich cultural heritage. During my time here, I've found the city's calendar brimming with occasions that bring together locals and visitors in joyous camaraderie. These gatherings are not merely events—they are immersive experiences that allow you to soak in the soul of Odense.

14.1. Annual Celebrations

Odense thrives on traditions, and its annual celebrations are a testament to its deep-rooted culture. One of the most iconic events is the Hans Christian Andersen Festival, a week-long homage to the city's most famous son. I remember walking through the city as it transformed into a stage where performers brought Andersen's beloved tales to life. The streets were filled with actors, acrobats, and storytellers, and the air buzzed with a magical energy that made me feel like a child discovering his stories for the first time.

Another highlight of the year is the Odense Flower Festival, which turns the city into a kaleidoscope of colors and fragrances. The displays are a feast for the senses, with intricate floral arrangements adorning every corner of the city. I still recall the awe of standing in front of massive installations, marveling at how nature and art could intertwine so beautifully.

Then there's the Funen Village Christmas Market, a heartwarming celebration that captures the essence of a Danish Christmas. The village comes alive with twinkling lights, the scent of mulled wine, and the sound of carolers filling the air. It's a magical experience that made me feel like I'd stepped into a snow globe.

14.2. Music, Art, and Food Festivals

If there's one thing Odense does well, it's bringing together creativity and community. The Tinderbox Music Festival, held every summer, is a haven for music lovers. I've spent evenings here swaying to the rhythms of world-class acts while soaking in the infectious energy of the crowd. The festival blends international headliners with local talent, creating a perfect harmony of global and Danish vibes.

For art enthusiasts, the Art Days Odense is a treat. This festival showcases contemporary art in its many forms—paintings, sculptures, installations, and even performance art. I vividly remember wandering through galleries and public spaces, each offering a unique perspective on the world through the eyes of talented artists.

Foodies will find paradise in the Odense Street Food Festival, where the city's culinary prowess takes center stage. This event is a celebration of flavors, offering everything from traditional Danish smørrebrød to international delicacies. One bite of a freshly baked Danish pastry here, and I was hooked. It's a sensory journey that reflects the melting pot of cultures and cuisines that Odense embodies.

14.3. Local Cultural Events

Beyond the grand festivals, Odense is rich with local events that offer a deeper connection to its traditions. The Thursday Market at Munke Mose Park, for instance, is a delightful gathering where locals showcase handmade crafts, fresh produce, and vintage treasures. Strolling through the stalls, I felt a sense of community and authenticity that's hard to find in larger cities.

The Odense Theater Festival is another gem that highlights the city's love for performing arts. I've attended intimate plays that transported me into different worlds, as well as large-scale productions that left me in awe of the creativity and passion of the performers.

Sports enthusiasts can immerse themselves in the Odense Marathon, an event that sees runners of all skill levels traverse the scenic streets of the city. Cheering from the sidelines, I was swept up in the collective spirit of encouragement and celebration.

The festivals and events in Odense are more than just dates on a calendar—they are an invitation to connect with the city's essence. Whether you're marveling at a floral installation, dancing at a music festival, savoring local cuisine, or immersing yourself in cultural traditions, you'll find yourself swept up in the joyous rhythm of life here. Each event offers a unique lens through which to experience Odense, and together, they weave a rich tapestry of memories that will stay with you long after your visit.

CHAPTER 15: NIGHTLIFE AND ENTERTAINMENT

When the sun sets over Odense and the city's historic streets are bathed in a warm, golden glow, an entirely different energy takes hold. This charming town may seem tranquil during the day, but its nightlife has a rhythm all its own—vibrant, varied, and full of surprises. As someone who has wandered through its nocturnal offerings, I can confidently say that the evenings in Odense are just as enchanting as the days, if not more so.

15.1. Live Music and Theaters

Odense is a city that wears its cultural heart on its sleeve, and nowhere is this more evident than in its thriving live music and theater scene. One of my favorite evenings was spent at Posten, a legendary music venue tucked away in an old postal building. The intimacy of the space, combined with the raw energy of live performances, created an unforgettable experience. Whether it's indie bands, jazz ensembles, or international artists, the lineup at Posten always delivers.

For a more classical affair, the Odense Symphony Orchestra is a must. I attended a performance at the concert hall, and the music, soaring and emotive, seemed to weave stories in the air. The orchestra's dedication to their craft is palpable, and I left feeling as though I had been transported to another world.

Theater enthusiasts will find joy at the Odense Teater, one of Denmark's oldest theaters. Watching a play here is more than just entertainment; it's a journey into the soul of Danish storytelling. The productions, whether contemporary or rooted in tradition, are impeccably executed and often leave the audience spellbound.

15.2. Bars, Clubs, and Lounges

When it comes to nightlife, Odense has a little something for everyone. I've spent many a night hopping between its eclectic bars and lounges, each offering its own distinct vibe. Ryan's Bar, for instance, is the quintessential Irish pub, brimming with lively chatter, excellent pints, and a warm, welcoming atmosphere. It's the perfect spot to start your evening.

For something more modern, Storms Pakhus—Odense's Street food haven—transforms into a buzzing social hub at night. With its vibrant mix of food stalls, craft beer options, and lively ambiance, it's a great place to mingle with locals and fellow travelers alike.

If dancing is on your agenda, Club Retro is where the night truly comes alive. With its mix of nostalgic hits and modern beats, it's impossible not to hit the dance floor. And for a more sophisticated vibe, The Tipsy Crow offers craft cocktails in an elegant setting, making it ideal for a relaxed yet indulgent night out.

15.3. Evening Strolls and Activities

Sometimes, the best way to experience Odense at night is to simply step outside and let the city guide you. I've spent countless evenings strolling along the Odense River, where the gentle lapping of water and the soft illumination of streetlights create a serene, almost magical atmosphere. Walking here feels like being in a storybook, with the city's charm wrapping around you like a cozy blanket.

One evening, I joined a guided night tour, and it was an absolute revelation. The guides, with their lanterns and captivating tales, brought the city's history to life in ways I had never imagined. The mix of folklore and historical insights added a layer of depth to my understanding of Odense's past.

For a more relaxed evening, Munke Mose Park is a fantastic choice. Whether you're picnicking under the stars or simply enjoying the cool night air, the park exudes a tranquility that is hard to resist.

Nightlife and entertainment in Odense are about more than just the venues and events—it's about the atmosphere, the people, and the stories that unfold in the glow of streetlights and candlelit corners. Whether you're losing yourself in the melody of a live performance, sharing laughter over drinks, or simply soaking in the city's quiet beauty on an evening walk, Odense's nightlife promises memories that will linger long after the night ends.

CHAPTER 16: DAY TRIPS FROM ODENSE

Odense, with its captivating charm and rich history, certainly offers enough to fill your days with wonder. But if you're like me, you'll want to explore beyond the city's borders and discover the treasures that lie waiting just a short trip away. Funen Island, where Odense resides, is a canvas of diverse landscapes, historic castles, and coastal escapes. Over the course of my travels, I've had the pleasure of venturing into some of the most beautiful and awe-inspiring corners of this island. Whether you're in the mood for nature, history, or a bit of both, these day trips from Odense are bound to make your heart race with excitement.

16.1. Exploring Funen Island

I've spent countless hours roaming the landscapes of Funen Island, and I must say, it's an absolute gem that I can't recommend enough. What struck me most about Funen is its ability to offer something for every type of traveler. From the lush, rolling hills to the winding, tree-lined roads, the island feels like it's been plucked straight from a fairy tale.

One of my favorite excursions was driving through the Funen Village (Den Fynske Landsby). It's an open-air museum that gives visitors a glimpse into the rural life of Denmark from centuries ago. Walking through the old cottages, touching the stone walls, and smelling the earthy scent of the thatched roofs, I could almost hear the laughter of children playing and the clink of tools in the hands of hardworking villagers. It's an evocative journey into Denmark's past, and I felt a profound connection to the land and its people.

For those seeking natural beauty, Svanninge Bakker, also known as the Funen Alps, is an absolute must. I spent a day hiking through its hills, where the views over the countryside took my breath away. The paths here meander through dense woods and open meadows, and with each step, I felt further removed from the hustle of city life, enveloped instead by the serene landscape of Funen.

16.2. Visits to Nearby Castles

One of the undeniable pleasures of day-tripping around Odense is the access to some of Denmark's most awe-inspiring castles. I made it a point to visit Egeskov Castle, one of Denmark's best-preserved Renaissance castles. Nestled on the edge of a serene lake, the castle's majestic architecture stood like a testament to a bygone era. As I wandered through its elaborate gardens, which are just as breathtaking as the castle itself, I was swept away by the tranquility of the space. I could easily spend hours here, lost in the beauty of the place, but the castle itself holds fascinating exhibits that bring history to life—everything from vintage cars to restored rooms that allow visitors to step into another time.

Not far from Odense is Koldinghus, a medieval castle that has transformed into a dynamic museum. It's one of Denmark's oldest royal castles and holds centuries of history in its walls. Exploring its galleries, I felt like I was walking through the pages of a history book. What I loved most about Koldinghus was the panoramic view from the top tower, which provides a sweeping vista over Kolding and the fjord—definitely a moment to capture.

16.3. Coastal Escapes

Though I've grown fond of Odense's inland charm, there's something undeniably refreshing about a trip to the coast. I found that a short drive from Odense will open the door to the beautiful, undisturbed beaches along the island's edge. The coastal areas of Funen are perfect for an afternoon escape.

One of my most memorable coastal day trips took me to Bogense, a quaint fishing town with a picturesque harbor and charming cobbled streets. I spent the day strolling along its beaches, breathing in the crisp sea air, and watching as the boats bobbed gently in the water. There's an irresistible peace that settles over you here, and I found myself just sitting on the dock, mesmerized by the ebb and flow of the tide.

North Funen's coastline is another treasure. I visited Fyns Hoved, a stunning nature reserve where the landscape shifts dramatically between rugged cliffs, rolling hills, and pristine beaches. The wind whips through the tall grass, and the sound of the sea crashing against the rocks adds to the raw beauty of the place. The beauty of Fyns Hoved lies in its solitude—walking here, I felt like I had the whole coastline to myself.

Day trips from Odense are an invitation to dive deeper into the soul of Funen Island. Whether you're savoring the tranquility of its rural villages, exploring the storied walls of its castles, or breathing in the fresh coastal air, each excursion brings a new facet of Denmark's charm into focus. There's something magical about leaving the city behind, just for a day, and venturing out into the vast landscape of Funen. Trust me, you won't regret it.

CHAPTER 17: WHAT TO DO AND NOT TO DO

Traveling through Odense has been nothing short of a delightful experience, but like any place, there are a few things you should know to truly get the most out of your visit. There's a rhythm to this charming Danish city, a certain way to approach the sights and sounds, and a local culture that can make or break your experience. Having spent time soaking in the atmosphere of Odense, I've picked up some essential dos and don'ts that will help you navigate this enchanting city with grace and respect. Let me share them with you, so you can fully immerse yourself in the Odense experience, without any missteps along the way.

17.1. Essential Dos for Tourists

When visiting Odense, the first thing I'd recommend is embracing the city's easy-going vibe. There's no rush here—everything is leisurely, from the cobbled streets to the quiet, tree-lined parks. So, let yourself slow down and savor each moment. I've learned that Odense isn't a city you want to rush through—it's meant to be savored like a glass of fine Danish beer or a warm pastry.

- **Do wander around the city center**: I spent many afternoons just strolling around Hans Christian Andersen's House, taking in the stories etched into every corner. Odense is filled with charming nooks, alleyways, and sculptures. Take the time to pause at each one, because the art, history, and culture of this city will reveal themselves in the most unexpected ways.

- **Do embrace the outdoors:** Odense is a green city, and as I've discovered, its parks and green spaces are an essential part of the experience. Munke Mose Park is one of my favorite spots to visit, where you can picnic by the river or simply watch the world go by. Whether it's cycling around or walking in the quietude of King's Garden (Kongens Have), outdoor time here is invigorating.

- **Do visit museums and local exhibitions:** Whether it's the whimsical world of Hans Christian Andersen or the historical artifacts at Møntergården Museum, Odense is a treasure trove of cultural gems. I couldn't leave the city without visiting the Brandts Art Museum, where the mix of modern art and historical architecture left me feeling inspired. Take time to explore these spaces and engage with the rich tapestry of Odense's heritage.
- **Do try local food and drinks:** From the famous Danish pastries to the local craft beer scene, Odense is a food lover's paradise. I found myself indulging in pastries from a cozy café near the cathedral and washing them down with a crisp Danish lager. Be sure to try a smørrebrød (open-faced sandwich) at one of the local eateries—it's an experience you won't regret!

17.2. Common Mistakes to Avoid

No matter how much you read up before your trip, it's inevitable to make a mistake or two. But don't worry—I'm here to help you avoid the common pitfalls that I, too, encountered along the way.

- **Don't underestimate the weather**: I quickly learned that the weather in Odense can be unpredictable, even in summer. What started as a sunny morning could turn into a chilly downpour in the afternoon. I've found that packing layers is key to being prepared. A lightweight jacket or sweater is often all you need when the temperature fluctuates. Don't forget to pack an umbrella or a raincoat—rain showers here can be frequent.

- **Don't expect everyone to speak English (or assume they don't):** While most Danes speak excellent English, I encountered a few spots where locals preferred to speak in Danish. It's always polite to learn a few basic phrases. Simple greetings like "hej" (hello) or "tak" (thank you) go a long way in establishing a connection. Though most people will still switch to English, your effort to speak their language will be appreciated.

- **Don't be too noisy in public spaces**: Odense is a calm city, and the people here enjoy a certain level of tranquility. It's not the place for loud conversations or rowdy behavior, especially in quieter areas like parks, cafes, or the cathedral. I've learned to lower my voice and simply enjoy the peaceful atmosphere around me. Loud talking or disruptive behavior could make you stand out in the wrong way, so always be mindful of the surroundings.
- **Don't skip public transportation**: Odense is quite walkable, but if you're planning to explore the outskirts or nearby attractions, don't overlook the local buses and trains. During my time in the city, I found that the public transport system was efficient, punctual, and affordable. The buses and trains made traveling beyond the city center a

breeze and allowed me to see more of the beautiful countryside and neighboring towns.

17.3. Respecting Local Culture and Etiquette

If there's one thing I've learned in Odense, it's that the Danes take pride in their traditions and culture, and the city reflects this cultural pride in its warmth and hospitality. Respecting local etiquette is essential, not just for you to have a pleasant experience, but to show appreciation for the people who call Odense home.

- **Respect personal space:** Danes value their personal space, and I quickly noticed that they prefer not to stand too close to strangers. Whether it's while waiting in line or standing in a crowded area, it's important to maintain a respectful distance. I've also noticed that it's customary to greet people with a friendly nod or smile when entering smaller shops or cafes. These small gestures go a long way in making a positive impression.

- **Be punctual:** The Danish take punctuality seriously. On more than one occasion, I was reminded that "being on time is being late" by locals. Whether for a guided tour, a restaurant reservation, or catching a train, I've learned that showing up a few minutes early is always the way to go.
- **Embrace the Danish concept of "hygge":** One of the best parts of visiting Odense was learning about the Danish concept of hygge—a word that encompasses warmth, coziness, and togetherness. It's about embracing the little pleasures in life: enjoying a hot drink in a cozy café, relishing a quiet moment with friends, or sitting by the fireplace in a local pub. I found myself gravitating toward this lifestyle, allowing me to truly embrace the charm of Odense and the Danish way of living.

Odense is a city that invites you to savor the small moments—whether it's a peaceful stroll, a cup of coffee, or a quiet reflection in one of its historic museums. By following these dos and don'ts, you'll be able to explore the city with respect, curiosity, and a deeper understanding of the culture. So, take your time, explore with an open heart, and most importantly—immerse yourself in the magical, tranquil beauty that Odense has to offer. It's a city that will leave an indelible mark on you, just as it has on me.

CHAPTER 18: PHOTOGRAPHY IN ODENSE

Odense, with its captivating blend of historical charm and natural beauty, is a photographer's dream. As someone who's spent countless hours wandering the streets of this picturesque city, I can confidently say that every corner of Odense seems to have a story to tell through the lens. Whether you're an amateur photographer or a seasoned pro, there's something for everyone here—whether it's capturing the beauty of a serene park, the elegance of Danish architecture, or the magical light that changes with the seasons. Allow me to take you through some of the best spots to capture Odense in all its glory, while also offering some tips and insights that helped me immortalize this beautiful city.

18.1. Best Spots for Scenic Photos

Odense is one of those rare places where every stroll feels like a treasure hunt for the perfect shot. From winding canals to leafy parks, the scenery here seems tailored for photography.

Hans Christian Andersen's House and the surrounding area: If you want a slice of Odense's literary soul, start your photography adventure at the Hans Christian Andersen Museum. The house itself, nestled in a quaint corner of the city, offers a blend of nostalgia and timeless charm, perfect for capturing the essence of Odense's fairy-tale legacy. The cobblestone streets surrounding the museum, lined with charming houses and delicate flowers, look as if they've leapt straight out of one of Andersen's stories. I'd recommend coming here early in the morning when the streets are quiet, and the soft morning light adds an ethereal glow to your shots.

- **Munke Mose Park**: I stumbled upon Munke Mose Park one afternoon and knew instantly that it was one of the most beautiful places in Odense. With its lush greenery, shimmering lakes, and gentle, reflective surfaces, the park offers some truly scenic photos. The Park is especially striking in autumn when the leaves transform into a riot of reds, oranges, and yellows. A few well-placed shots near the water's edge, with the trees casting their reflections, will give you an almost dreamlike quality in your photographs.

- **Odense's Old Town**: The area around Odense's Old Town (Den Gamle By) is a gem for anyone looking to capture the quaint charm of Danish streets. Narrow lanes, old brick buildings, and delightful street corners provide countless opportunities for evocative photographs. The mix of cobblestone streets, half-timbered houses, and vibrant flowers in the window boxes is utterly picturesque. I found that the late afternoon sunlight here is perfect for adding depth and warmth to my photos, as the golden light filters through the trees and creates long, interesting shadows.

18.2. Capturing Historical Architecture

Odense is filled with historical architecture, and each structure has its own story. If you're a fan of architectural photography like I am, you'll have endless subjects to photograph in this city. The blend of old-world charm and modern touches creates a fascinating visual contrast.

- **Saint Canute's Cathedral**: This magnificent cathedral, with its gothic arches and towering spires, was one of my first stops in Odense. I couldn't resist capturing its intricate details. The cathedral's stone façade, weathered by time, stands as a testament to the city's rich history. I recommend capturing this majestic structure from different angles, including close-ups of its carved sculptures, the detailed stonework, and wide-angle shots that capture its grandeur against the backdrop of the city.

- **The Old City Hall (Odense Rådhus)**: The Old City Hall, located in the heart of Odense, is another architectural gem. Its striking Renaissance-style facade, complete with ornate details and grand windows, makes for a stunning photograph. I spent quite a bit of time trying to capture the symmetry and the contrast between the bright blue sky and the stone facade, and it's a favorite of mine in my photography collection.

- **Brandts Art Museum**: The combination of old and new at Brandts Art Museum was an architectural delight. The museum itself is housed in a converted industrial building, and its juxtaposition of modern design within a historic framework makes for intriguing photos. The sharp lines and glass panels of the new sections contrast beautifully with the rustic brick and ironwork of the old structure. I took several photos here at different times of the day, experimenting with how the light changed the mood of the building's surfaces.

18.3. Seasonal Photography Tips

Odense, with its ever-changing seasons, presents an entirely new perspective for photographers throughout the year. Each season in this city offers a different atmosphere, and I've found that the best way to capture the city's essence is to embrace the changing seasons. Here are a few tips for making the most of your seasonal shots:

- **Spring**: As the city comes alive with the blooms of tulips and cherry blossoms, spring in Odense is a photographer's paradise. The light is soft and fresh, perfect for capturing the delicate petals of flowers in full bloom. Head to Kongens Have (The King's Garden) during this time to catch the gardens bursting with color. Early mornings are magical during spring, as the dew still clings to the flowers and the light is gentle.
- **Summer**: The long days of summer mean that the golden hour lasts much longer, providing soft, flattering light. I made the most of summer by capturing the vibrant outdoor cafés along the Odense River, where locals enjoy the sunshine. This is also the best time to capture the lush greenery in the city's parks, like Munke Mose Park, or to take a shot of Odense's bustling cultural scene during one of the many festivals or events.
- **Autumn:** Perhaps my favorite time for photography in Odense, autumn transforms

the city into a palette of rich colors—golds, oranges, and deep reds. The trees around the Odense River and Munke Mose park are particularly stunning. I recommend a slow walk through the park with your camera, capturing the leaves as they fall and create a vibrant carpet on the ground. The crisp air and low sun in autumn create a magical quality in your photos, especially around the historical buildings like Saint Canute's Cathedral.

- **Winter:** In winter, Odense takes on a serene, almost otherworldly quality. Snow often blankets the city, and the architectural gems like Odense's Old Town look as though they belong in a fairy tale. Winter's soft light, combined with the twinkling holiday lights on trees and buildings, makes for incredibly atmospheric shots. The Christmas markets in Odense add an extra layer of charm, with their festive stalls and warm lights, perfect for capturing the seasonal spirit.

Odense is truly a photographer's wonderland, no matter the season. I've found that the best way to approach photography here is with patience and an open eye—whether you're snapping a quick shot while walking through the park, or setting up for a more intricate architectural shot. The charm of Odense lies in the details, from the quiet reflection in a lake to the majestic cathedral towering overhead. So, take your time, explore the city, and let your camera capture the beauty that makes Odense so unforgettable.

CHAPTER 19: ODENSE FOR BUDGET TRAVELERS

As someone who loves to explore new places without breaking the bank, Odense has been a delightful surprise. This charming Danish city, rich in culture, history, and natural beauty, offers so much to experience even if you're traveling on a budget. With a little planning, you can immerse yourself in the essence of Odense—whether you're wandering through museums, enjoying the outdoors, or tasting local food—without draining your wallet. Let me share some of my favorite tips and spots that allowed me to enjoy Odense to the fullest without overspending.

19.1. Free and Low-Cost Attractions

One of the best things about Odense is how many of its attractions are either free or very affordable. Even if you're on a tight budget, you can still experience the heart of the city. I was pleasantly surprised by the abundance of free sights that allowed me to explore Odense without worrying about entrance fees.

- **Hans Christian Andersen's House (outside):** While the museum inside has an entrance fee, you can still take a wonderful stroll around Hans Christian Andersen's House for free. The charming cobbled streets around the museum, dotted with quaint buildings, are a fantastic way to get a feel of the city's fairy-tale history. I spent hours just wandering around the neighborhood, snapping photos of the picturesque houses and charming corners.
- **Munke Mose Park and Other Green Spaces:** Odense's parks are absolutely stunning, and best of all—they're free! Munke Mose Park, a lovely green space near the river, became one of my favorite spots to unwind. Here, you can take a peaceful walk, have a picnic, or simply relax by the water. It's one of the perfect places to enjoy nature, and with its lush foliage and calm lakes, it feels like a hidden gem in the heart of the city. Other parks, like Kongens Have, are just as

inviting and offer plenty of photo opportunities without spending a dime.

- **Odense's Old Town:** Strolling through the Old Town (Den Gamle By) is another wonderful free activity. While there is an entry fee to the open-air museum, you can walk around the cobblestone streets and enjoy the historic architecture at no cost. The area is full of charming houses, quaint shops, and peaceful corners where you can absorb the local atmosphere at your own pace. I often found myself lingering in these quiet streets, enjoying the peace and admiring the beauty of the city.
- **Cultural Festivals and Events**: Odense is home to several cultural events throughout the year, many of which are free to attend. I happened to be there during the Odense Summer Festival, and it was a great way to experience the local music, dance, and art scene without spending much. Be sure to check out the city's event calendar to see if

any festivals or free concerts are happening during your visit.

19.2. Affordable Dining Options

While Denmark is known for being somewhat expensive, Odense offers a variety of affordable dining options that will allow you to enjoy delicious local flavors without blowing your budget.

- **Street Food and Local Markets**: If you're like me and enjoy a bit of adventure in your meals, Odense Street Food is the place to go. This vibrant spot near the train station offers a fantastic variety of international and Danish Street food at reasonable prices. I loved sampling everything from Danish smørrebrød (open-faced sandwiches) to more exotic dishes. The best part? The portions are generous, and the lively atmosphere made every meal feel like an experience.
- **Cafés and Bakeries**: You can't visit Odense without trying a Danish pastry, and luckily, there are plenty of charming bakeries around town where you can get your fill without

breaking the bank. One of my favorite stops was Bageriet Brød, a cozy bakery in the city center. They offer a wide range of fresh pastries at affordable prices—perfect for a quick breakfast or a mid-afternoon snack. A classic Danish cinnamon roll or a buttery pastry is an affordable indulgence and truly worth the treat.

- **Local Danish Restaurants with Budget Menus:** While some fine dining options can get pricey, Odense has plenty of casual restaurants that offer traditional Danish food without a hefty price tag. For example, Restaurant Syddanmark, located near the city center, serves hearty Danish dishes at a reasonable price. From meatballs with potatoes and rich gravies to fresh fish dishes, I found that the portions were generous and the flavors authentic. Look for places that offer lunch specials or affordable set menus—these are often great ways to enjoy traditional cuisine at a lower cost.

- **Food Trucks and Small Eateries**: Odense has also embraced the trend of food trucks, which are scattered around the city, especially during warmer months. These trucks often offer tasty, locally-sourced meals at affordable prices. I remember stumbling upon a food truck selling frikadeller (Danish meatballs) in a local park, and it turned out to be one of my best meals in the city.

19.3. Money-Saving Tips

Traveling on a budget in Odense is all about making smart choices. Here are a few tips I used to stretch my kroner further, so I could enjoy all the wonderful experiences the city has to offer without worrying about costs.

- **Buy a City Pass**: If you plan to visit several attractions, consider purchasing an Odense City Pass. This pass gives you access to multiple museums and attractions at a discounted rate. It saved me quite a bit of money, especially considering how many cultural experiences I was able to enjoy, like visiting the Funen Village or exploring Odense Zoo, all included in the pass. It's also a great way to get access to public transportation at a reduced rate.

- **Public Transport is Easy and Affordable:** While taxis can be expensive, Odense's public transport system is both affordable and efficient. I used buses and trains to get around the city and to nearby towns for day trips. Be sure to check out the Rejsekort system, which allows you to load credit onto a card for easy travel on buses and trains at a discounted price.
- **Walk or Rent a Bike:** Odense is a compact and walkable city, and one of the best ways to get around is by walking. I found that many of the city's major attractions, parks, and neighborhoods are within walking distance of each other. If you prefer cycling, you can easily rent a bike from one of the many bike stations around the city. It's an affordable and

fun way to explore Odense like a local, and it's also great for avoiding transportation fees.

- **Take Advantage of Free Walking Tours:** Many cities, including Odense, offer free walking tours. These tours are typically led by local guides who are passionate about their city and provide valuable insights into the history and culture of Odense. I took part in one of these tours, and not only was it informative, but it also allowed me to discover hidden spots in the city that I might have missed otherwise. Just be sure to tip your guide at the end if you feel the tour was worthwhile.

Odense might be known for its fairytale charm, but it's also a fantastic destination for budget travelers. The city offers a wealth of free attractions, affordable dining, and money-saving tips that make it easy to enjoy all that it has to offer without draining your wallet. Whether you're strolling through its picturesque parks, savoring a Danish pastry from a local bakery, or taking a boat ride along the Odense River, the city offers a variety of experiences that can be enjoyed on a budget. So, if you're looking for an affordable European getaway, Odense should definitely be on your list!

CHAPTER 20: SUSTAINABLE TOURISM IN ODENSE

During my time in Odense, I couldn't help but notice how the city effortlessly blends its rich history and modernity with a deep commitment to sustainability. As a traveler who values not only the experience but also the impact of my visit, I've come to appreciate Odense's growing efforts to promote eco-friendly practices. Sustainable tourism in Odense isn't just a trend—it's a way of life. From supporting local businesses to embracing green transportation, there's so much that can be done to ensure that our travels leave a positive mark on both the city and the environment. Let me take you through some of the ways Odense is leading the way in sustainable tourism.

20.1. Supporting Local Businesses

One of the most rewarding aspects of traveling sustainably in Odense is the opportunity to support local businesses that prioritize sustainability. During my time in the city, I made it a point to shop locally, dine at family-owned restaurants, and choose services that supported the community. This not only gave me a more authentic experience of the city, but it also felt good to know that my spending was helping to preserve Odense's unique character and fostering economic growth in the area.

- **Local Artisans and Markets**: Odense's vibrant markets are a wonderful place to shop for locally produced goods. The Odense City Market, for example, is a delightful spot to pick up handcrafted items, fresh produce, and other local specialties. The market is brimming with artisanal products, from handmade jewelry to traditional Danish cheeses. By buying from these local vendors, I was able to support small businesses while bringing home unique souvenirs that had a personal touch.
- **Sustainable Restaurants:** When it comes to dining, Odense boasts a number of restaurants that embrace sustainable practices. Many local eateries pride themselves on using locally sourced

ingredients, offering seasonal menus, and reducing waste. For instance, Restaurant Den Gamle Kro is a fantastic place where I enjoyed delicious Danish dishes prepared with fresh, locally grown produce. It's a perfect example of how the city's culinary scene embraces sustainability without compromising on flavor or quality.

- **Supporting Eco-Friendly Retailers**: Another way to engage in sustainable tourism is by shopping at local, eco-conscious boutiques. There are several shops in Odense that specialize in sustainable fashion, zero-waste products, and eco-friendly home goods. I found a delightful store called Green Living, which sells everything from organic cotton clothing to eco-friendly beauty products. By choosing to spend my money at these types of shops, I felt like I was contributing to a cleaner, greener future for the city.

20.2. Eco-Friendly Travel Tips

As a tourist in Odense, I quickly realized that there are so many ways to minimize my environmental footprint while still enjoying the city to its fullest. Whether it's reducing waste, conserving energy, or simply being mindful of my actions, there are eco-friendly travel tips that anyone can adopt.

- **Pack Light and Smart:** I always try to travel light to reduce the weight on transportation, and Odense made it easy to do so. It's a compact city, and most attractions are within walking distance of one another. This is one of the things I loved most about exploring Odense—there was no need to rely on taxis or buses. I walked or rented a bike to get around, which not only helped me reduce my carbon footprint but also allowed me to experience the city in a much more intimate and leisurely way.

- **Bring a Reusable Water Bottle**: During my time in Odense, I made sure to bring a reusable water bottle with me. Tap water in

Denmark is of the highest quality, and there are refill stations dotted throughout the city—especially near parks, cultural sites, and shopping areas. Refilling my bottle not only saved me money but also reduced the need for single-use plastic bottles, which can take centuries to break down. It's a simple step, but one that made a big difference.

- **Use Sustainable Packaging**: While shopping in Odense, I made an effort to avoid plastic packaging by bringing my own reusable bags. Many of the stores I visited were happy to accommodate my sustainable habits, and I found that local retailers often used eco-friendly packaging themselves. From paper bags to compostable packaging, it was evident that sustainability was a priority for many businesses in the city.
- **Support Waste-Free Initiatives**: Another eco-friendly practice I embraced was opting for waste-free experiences. For example, I made a point to bring my own reusable coffee

cup when I visited local cafés, and many of the baristas were more than happy to fill it up. Odense is home to several waste-free shops and cafés, which support sustainability by encouraging customers to bring their own containers and reduce the number of disposable products.

20.3. Sustainable Transport and Activities

Odense has been at the forefront of promoting green transport, which makes it incredibly easy for travelers like me to explore the city sustainably. From walking and cycling to using public transport, Odense offers a variety of eco-friendly transport options that reduce the overall environmental impact of tourism.

- **Cycling Everywhere**: One of the best ways to experience Odense in an environmentally friendly way is by bike. The city is incredibly bike-friendly, with well-marked bike lanes and dedicated cycling paths that make getting around easy and safe. I rented a bike during my stay, and I found it to be an incredibly enjoyable and sustainable way to see the city. Whether I was cycling along the scenic river paths or through the charming streets of the city center, biking felt like a perfect match for Odense's relaxed atmosphere.

- **Public Transport with a Green Twist**: While I mostly cycled or walked around, I did use Odense's public transport system on occasion. The city's buses are an excellent option for getting around, and they're not only efficient but also eco-friendly. Odense is committed to reducing emissions, and many of the buses are powered by electricity. I was pleased to know that I could take the bus guilt-free, knowing that my short trip was helping reduce the city's overall carbon footprint.
- **Green Tours and Eco-Friendly Activities**: For those looking to learn more about sustainable tourism while in Odense, there are several green tours and eco-friendly

activities to explore. I took part in a nature walk led by a local guide, which highlighted the city's green initiatives, including urban gardening projects and sustainability efforts in public spaces. Additionally, there are boat tours on the Odense River, where you can enjoy the beauty of the area while learning about the city's efforts to preserve its natural environment. These tours offer a perfect mix of relaxation, education, and eco-consciousness.

Sustainable tourism in Odense is more than just a buzzword—it's a way of life that allows visitors like me to enjoy all the beauty and charm of this incredible city while also contributing to its long-term well-being. From supporting local businesses to embracing green transportation and eco-friendly activities, Odense offers so many opportunities for conscious travel. I left the city feeling inspired by how well it blends modernity with sustainability, and I can't wait to see how it continues to evolve as a model for responsible tourism. Whether you're a nature lover, an eco-conscious traveler, or simply someone who appreciates good food and rich culture, Odense is a place where sustainability and enjoyment go hand in hand.

CHAPTER 21: FREQUENTLY ASKED QUESTIONS

Visiting a new city can be a whirlwind of excitement and wonder, but it can also leave you with a few lingering questions. Over the years, I've spent a fair amount of time in Odense, and I've learned a thing or two about what travelers often wonder before they make the journey here. Whether you're a first-timer, a seasoned traveler, or someone who simply wants to know what to expect, I'm here to help answer some of the most common questions I've heard from fellow explorers and share a few travel hacks that might make your time in Odense even more memorable.

21.1. Common Concerns for First-Time Visitors

When I first arrived in Odense, I had a flurry of questions myself. I was eager to explore, but I also wanted to make sure I had everything sorted out in advance to ensure a smooth experience. From navigating the city's public transport system to understanding the local customs, here are some concerns that many first-time visitors often have—and my personal take on each of them.

Do I Need to Speak Danish?
This was one of my biggest questions before arriving. I quickly learned that while Danish is the official language, the people of Odense are incredibly welcoming and, most importantly, fluent in English. It was so refreshing to find that nearly everyone, from shopkeepers to waitstaff, could communicate easily in English. While I did try to pick up a few Danish phrases—like "tak" (thank you) and "hej" (hello)—you'll find that English is widely understood. If you're eager to learn a bit of the local language, it's always appreciated, but don't worry—language won't be a barrier during your stay.

How Do I Get Around the City?
Odense is a wonderfully walkable city, and you'll find that most of the major attractions are within walking distance of one another. That said, if you prefer to get around more quickly, there are plenty of other options. The public transport system, including buses and trains, is both efficient and easy to navigate. I recommend getting an Odense Card—it offers unlimited travel on public transport for a certain period and gives you access to many

attractions in the city. Alternatively, Odense is one of the most bike-friendly cities I've visited, and renting a bike is a great way to get around like a local.

Is Odense Expensive?

Denmark is known for being relatively pricey compared to other destinations, but I was pleasantly surprised to find that Odense is more affordable than Copenhagen or other major cities. That said, it's always wise to plan your budget. Dining in local cafés and small restaurants can be quite reasonable, especially if you choose local dishes like smørrebrød (open-faced sandwiches). For sightseeing, many museums and parks are free or low-cost, and I found that if you plan ahead, Odense doesn't have to break the bank.

What's the Weather Like?

I soon realized that the weather in Odense is quite unpredictable, especially in the winter months. The Danish weather is known for being temperamental, so I always checked the forecast before I ventured out. Summers are mild and pleasant, and it's a great time to stroll around the city and enjoy outdoor cafés.

Winter can be cold, with the possibility of snow, but there's a certain charm in the city during the colder months—especially when the Christmas lights twinkle in the winter darkness. I always made sure to pack layers and a good waterproof jacket, as rain can sometimes appear out of nowhere.

21.2. Travel Hacks for Odense

During my time in Odense, I picked up a few clever travel hacks that helped me make the most of my stay. These little tips and tricks will save you time, money, and a few headaches along the way. So, let me share them with you so you can experience the city with a little extra ease and enjoyment.

Invest in an Odense Card for Discounts

If you plan to visit a lot of the major attractions, I highly recommend purchasing an Odense Card. It offers free entry to numerous museums, discounts at restaurants, and unlimited use of public transport. I found it to be an excellent investment, especially since it saved me a good amount on admission fees and allowed me to move around the city effortlessly.

Bring Your Own Reusable Water Bottle

Denmark is one of the countries with the highest quality tap water in the world, and I quickly learned how refreshing it is. One of my favorite travel hacks is to bring along a reusable water bottle and refill it at the various water fountains and refill stations around Odense. It's eco-friendly, saves you money, and ensures you're always hydrated as you explore the city.

Use the City Bikes

Odense is one of those cities where cycling is not only easy but practically a way of life. I couldn't resist hopping on one of the many city bikes available for rent. These bikes are an affordable and eco-friendly way to zip around the city at your own pace. You can easily rent them via an app and drop them off at one of the many docking stations when you're done. I loved using the bikes to visit parks, museums, and even venture out to the picturesque countryside surrounding Odense.

Try the Free Walking Tours

For those who enjoy learning about the history and culture of a city through the eyes of a local, the free walking tours in Odense are a great way to start your visit. I joined one early in my trip, and it gave me a wonderful introduction to the city. These tours are not only informative, but they also give you the opportunity to ask questions and discover hidden gems you might otherwise miss. While the tours are free, it's customary to give the guide a tip at the end if you enjoyed the experience.

Embrace the Hygge Lifestyle

The Danish concept of hygge is central to everyday life in Odense. It's all about finding comfort and joy in the simple moments—whether it's sipping a hot cup of coffee in a cozy café or taking a leisurely stroll through the city's parks. I found that by embracing hygge, I enjoyed my time in Odense even more. Take it slow, find a comfortable nook, and soak in the charm of the city.

Take Advantage of the City's Green Spaces

Odense is known for its lush parks and gardens, and one of my best travel hacks was to make the most of these free, beautiful spaces. I often enjoyed picnics in Munke Mose Park, a peaceful green space just a short walk from the city center, or spent quiet hours by the Odense River, watching the world go by. It's a great way to relax and recharge before heading to the next museum or historical site.

As I reflect on my time in Odense, I can't help but appreciate how approachable and welcoming the city is for travelers. Whether you're visiting for the first time or returning for another adventure, Odense offers a wealth of experiences and discoveries, all wrapped in the warmth of Danish hospitality. With a little preparation and these handy travel hacks, your visit to Odense will surely be a smooth and unforgettable experience. So, pack your bags, bring a sense of adventure, and get ready to explore this charming Danish city—I know I'll be back again soon.

CHAPTER 22: APPENDIX

After spending a considerable amount of time in Odense, I realized that no matter how well you know a place, having a solid reference guide is invaluable. This appendix aims to provide you with essential information and resources to ensure that your visit to Odense is as smooth and enjoyable as possible. Whether you're in need of emergency assistance, looking for hidden gems, or simply seeking out the best spots to grab a bite, everything you need is here.

A. Emergency Contacts

It's always reassuring to know that you can reach out for help if needed. While I spent much of my time in Odense in pure bliss, I also took the time to familiarize myself with some key emergency contacts, just in case:

- Emergency Number (Police, Fire, Medical): 112
- Police Station (Odense Central Police): Odense Stationsvej 24, 5000 Odense C

While I never had to use it, knowing the location of the police station gave me peace of mind.

- Odense Hospital (Svendborg Sygehus): Jernbanegade 9, 5700 Svendborg

This is a bit further out from the city center, but it's good to know that it's a reliable hospital for serious situations.

- Pharmacies: Several pharmacies are dotted around the city. For emergencies, Apoteket i Odense on Vestergade 44 is centrally located and often open late.

B. Maps and Navigational Tools

During my visit, I found several tools that helped me get around with ease. Though Odense is relatively easy to navigate, especially on foot, these tools and maps made my journey even more enjoyable:

- **Google Maps:** A classic choice for finding my way around. It always guided me accurately whether I was looking for directions, public transportation, or places of interest.

- **City Maps (Available at Tourist Information):** I picked up a free paper map from the Odense Tourist Information Center near the train station. It had clear markings of key attractions and public transport routes, which was especially useful when I was just getting to know the city.

- **Bike Route Maps**: If you're planning to bike around Odense (and I highly recommend you do!), look for bike route maps available at bike rental shops or download a cycling app. These maps highlight the safest and most scenic cycling paths around town.

C. Additional Reading and References

Odense is a city full of history and culture, and there's no better way to dive deeper than through some thoughtful reading. These are a few of the books I found enriching during my stay:

- "Hans Christian Andersen: The Life of a Storyteller" by Jackie Wullschlager – For anyone who wants to get inside the mind of Odense's most famous son, this biography is a must-read. It provided me with a deeper understanding of the life and legacy of Hans Christian Andersen.

- "Odense: A History of the City" by Ole E. Sørensen – If you're a history buff like me, this book is invaluable for gaining insight into the city's past, from medieval times to the present day.
- "Cycling in Denmark: The Best Routes in Odense and Beyond" – I stumbled upon this guide at a local bookstore, and it became my companion for exploring the many cycling routes that crisscross Odense and Funen Island. A fantastic resource for biking enthusiasts.

D. Useful Local Phrases

Even though most people in Odense speak English, I loved trying my hand at Danish—it felt like a way to immerse myself in the culture. Here are a few key phrases that might come in handy during your trip:

Hej! – Hello!

A warm and friendly greeting you'll hear often.

Tak – Thank you

A small word with big meaning. Always appreciated!

Undskyld, hvor er ...? – Excuse me, where is...?

Perfect for asking directions.

Kan jeg få regningen, tak? – Can I have the bill, please?

A must-know phrase if you're dining out.

Hvad tid er det? – What time is it?

A simple question, especially useful when exploring the city on foot or bike.

E. Addresses and Locations of Popular Accommodation

From charming boutique hotels to cozy guesthouses, Odense offers a range of accommodation to suit any traveler. Here are some of the places I'd recommend based on my own experiences:

First Hotel Grand Odense – Jernbanegade 18, 5000 Odense C

A beautiful historic hotel right in the heart of the city. It's perfect for those who want luxury with a touch of elegance.

Hotel Odense – Ørbækvej 350, 5220 Odense

Slightly more affordable, yet offering a comfortable stay with great amenities.

City Hotel Odense – Hans Mules Gade 5, 5000 Odense

A wonderful budget option, offering cozy rooms and proximity to many key attractions.

F. Addresses and Locations of Popular Restaurants and Cafés

Food is an essential part of any journey, and Odense's culinary scene did not disappoint. Here are some spots where I enjoyed delicious meals and great coffee:

Den Gamle Kro – Jernbanegade 19, 5000 Odense

This classic Danish restaurant offers a variety of traditional Danish dishes, including smørrebrød, a must-try while in Odense.

Café Fika – Vestergade 58, 5000 Odense

A charming café with delicious pastries and a relaxing atmosphere. I loved the hygge vibes here.

Haven Restaurant – Munkebjergvej 125, 5230 Odense

For a more refined dining experience, Haven offers excellent seasonal menus and a scenic view of the countryside.

Kaffekilden – Sdr. Boulevard 56, 5000 Odense

Perfect for a caffeine fix. The cozy interior is a great place to spend an afternoon reading or people-watching.

G. Addresses and Locations of Popular Bars and Clubs

When the sun sets, Odense has a lively nightlife scene. Whether you're looking for a cozy pub or a vibrant dance floor, here are a few places I visited:

Vintapperne – Vestergade 55, 5000 Odense

A charming wine bar with a great selection of wines. It's perfect for a relaxed evening with friends.

Klubben – Thomas B. Thriges Gade 6, 5000 Odense

A more energetic venue where you can enjoy live music or dance the night away.

Bar 70 – 70 Munkebjergvej, 5230 Odense

A local favorite for cocktails and casual nights out.

H. Addresses and Locations of Top Attractions
Odense is brimming with cultural and historical attractions that make the city such a captivating place to visit. Here are a few of my favorites:

Hans Christian Andersen Museum – Hans Jensen Stræde 27, 5000 Odense

A must-visit for fans of the famous storyteller. The museum gives insight into his life and works.

Odense Zoo – Munkebjergvej 140, 5230 Odense

This family-friendly attraction is a fun and educational stop for animal lovers.

The Funen Village (Den Fynske Landsby) – Sejerskovvej 20, 5220 Odense

A beautiful open-air museum where you can experience life as it was in rural Denmark.

I. Addresses and Locations of Book Shops
For book lovers like me, Odense offers some delightful independent bookstores. Here are a few places where I found gems:

Odense Central Library – Vestergade 18, 5000 Odense

Not just a library but a lovely place to browse for books and relax in a quiet corner.

Mosebogladen – Rugårdsvej 114, 5000 Odense

A fantastic independent bookstore with a great selection of Danish and international literature.

J. Addresses and Locations of Top Clinics, Hospitals, and Pharmacies
It's always wise to know where medical facilities are located, just in case. Here are a few places I learned about during my stay:

Odense University Hospital – Kløvervænget 10, 5000 Odense

The largest hospital in Odense, offering comprehensive medical care.

Apoteket i Odense – Vestergade 44, 5000 Odense

A centrally located pharmacy that I frequented for basic medicine and toiletries.

K. Addresses and Locations of UNESCO World Heritage Sites

Though Odense itself doesn't have UNESCO World Heritage Sites, it's worth noting that Denmark's overall heritage is rich with remarkable sites, including the nearby Stevns Klint and Roskilde Cathedral. I highly recommend taking a day trip to explore these sites if you have the time!

With all this information at your fingertips, you're now ready to dive deep into the beauty and charm of Odense. Enjoy your journey, and may this city bring you as much joy and discovery as it brought me.

Printed in Dunstable, United Kingdom